THE SW

A HISTORY OF THE HOLY RIVER OF ST PAULINUS

C000283700

ID
13

Cover illustrations:
Front: *Wain Wath falls, River Swale, Swaledale*
(PHOTO: TOM PARKER)
Back: *The Swale below Low Row*

If fate compels me to leave this dear spot
And in other lands far away roam
My earnest wish whate'r be my lot
Is to end my days here at home.

Words taken from the Song of Swaledale

THE SWALE

A HISTORY OF
THE HOLY RIVER OF
ST PAULINUS

by

David Morris

William Sessions Limited
York, England

© David Morris 1994

First printed 1994
Revised second edition 1995
Reprinted 1999

ISBN 1 85072 173 4

By the same author:
The Dalesmen of the Mississippi River

Printed in 11 on 14 point
New Century Schoolbook Typeface
from Author's Disk
by William Sessions Limited
The Ebor Press
York, England

The Historic River Swale

THE ANGLO-SAXONS CALLED it 'Sualuae' meaning rapid and liable to deluge, an apt description of a river which rises in the high Pennines and over a distance of some seventy miles, falls steeply down towards the lower levels of the Vale of York. There it joins with the River Ure to form the Ouse which then flows onwards to York and to the Humber estuary beyond.

In the days of Paulinus, the Swale was described as 'a Holy River' and even 'The Jordan of England'. Today, the beauty of the Swale is always an attraction but it is a river with such a wealth of history over so many centuries that its story surely deserves to be told.

Acknowledgements

IN THE PREPARATION OF this book I have received invaluable assistance from many sources and my thanks are due to all those who have helped with information and advice. Some must be given particular mention.

Peter Cardwell for advice on the Medieval Hospital of St Giles and Cataractonium.

Rosemary Cramp for information about Bainesse Farm and Cataractonium.

Jane Hatcher for her guidance regarding Richmond and its history.

Tim Laurie for information about the Swaledale Ancient Land Boundaries Project.

Mollie Squires for her historical assistance.

Ralph Waggett for his considerable knowledge of Swaledale and its people.

Julie Bowman for her map drawing.

Contents

Illustrations and Maps

CHAPTER I

The Birth of the River

HIGH ABOVE THE VILLAGE of Keld in Upper Swaledale is a hill-top known as Hugh Seat. It is one of the highest points of a long ridge of hills standing steeply above Mallerstang and forming a natural boundary between Cumbria and North Yorkshire. On a clear day, Hugh Seat, with its lofty neighbour High Seat, provide a magnificent view westwards to the peaks of the Lake District and to the sea beyond. To the east lies an amphitheatre once lined with a forest of birch trees. It is here that waters have for long collected to form the Birkdale and Sleddale becks. Together they provide the source of the River Swale.

Hugh Seat, from which rises the Great Sleddale Beck, was named after Hugh de Morville, a local landowner of the 12th century. His name is not always regarded in historical records with much favour mainly because he is thought to have taken part in the murder of Saint Thomas

1. *Lady Anne's Stone Pillar on which are carved her initials 'A.P.' and the year 1664.*

1

Becket. Those who climb Hugh Seat however remember the name of quite a different person, an extraordinary lady of northern history who lived some five centuries after Hugh de Morville. She is the Lady Anne Clifford, Countess of Dorset and Pembroke. Inset in a pillar built on a cairn beyond Hugh Seat is a stone bearing her initials and the year 1664. This was the year when, at the age of 74, she is reported to have 'ridden the bounds' of her estate passing along the ridge and over Hugh Seat.

Lady Anne was the only daughter of George Clifford the third Earl of Cumberland and Lady Margaret Russell, who were married in 1577. There were two other children, both boys who died at an early age. Anne was born in Skipton Castle in January 1590 and was to live over a span of eighty-six eventful years through the reigns of Elizabeth I, James I, Charles I, Cromwell and Charles II. Fortunately, she was a great diary keeper and her records in the shape of four separate manuscripts give an insight into over seventy years of her long life.

Her father, the Earl of Cumberland, did little to aid Lady Anne's upbringing and it was left to her mother to devote much time to Anne's education and welfare. They were in London at the time of Queen Elizabeth's death and, in her diary, Anne recorded that she was forbidden to attend the Westminster funeral because she was too small. However, she wanted to go, and in the end she got her way as she often did in later life. Sadly, her marriages brought her problems and little happiness. Her first husband who became the Earl of Dorset proved to be a great spender, they drifted apart and he died in 1624. Her second marriage was to Philip Earl of Pembroke who proved to be callous and quite unsuitable as a husband. He died in 1650.

On the death of Lady Anne's father at the age of 47 his estates would normally have passed to Anne as his only surviving child, but they were left instead to the Earl's younger

2

2. *Lady Anne Clifford, Countess of Dorset and Pembroke.*
(FROM THE NATIONAL PORTRAIT GALLERY PICTURE LIBRARY)

3

brother Francis. Anne's mother Lady Clifford, to whom she was very devoted, went to live at Brougham Castle and being concerned for her daughter, she spent much of her widowhood studying the historical and legal background of the Clifford inheritance. It was not until 1644 that Francis died and Lady Anne at last succeeded to the family estates. They included the castles at Brougham, Appleby, Brough, Pendragon and Skipton, where Anne was born. Lady Anne was to spend all her many remaining years maintaining her estate and working for the welfare of her community. She was deeply religious and very attached to her family and she is remembered today as a great lady of her time, a woman whose undoubted strength of character was mixed with humility and consideration for others less fortunate than herself.

When Lady Anne rode over her estate boundaries and came to Hugh Seat she would have seen to the east the Great Sleddale Beck and the whole amphitheatre which provides the source of the River Swale. She would see the massive slopes of Great Shunner Fell, the Norse name for which was 'Sjonar' meaning a look-out hill, and to the north, the border hill with the rather extraordinary name of Nine Standards Rigg. Close to the county boundary, it stands 2,170 feet high and, though their purpose remains uncertain, local legend tells us that the nine standards, which are dry stone pillars, were constructed at the time of the marauding Scots. It was hoped that the Scottish raiders would mistake them for the standard bearers of a considerable defending army and would retreat whence they came. Though this could have been the purpose of the pillars, history cannot be said to confirm that they had the desired effect.

Across the amphitheatre before her, Lady Anne might well have seen the waters of a tarn high up on Birkdale Common, 1600 feet above sea level. There always seems to have been a tarn there though during the last century it was dammed at one end to build up the water and help serve the local lead mines. Rarely visited by walkers, Birkdale tarn stands today remote, its waters broken by the Pennine winds and its peace disturbed only by the calls of gulls and other birds of the Common.

Far below is Birkdale Beck formed when the Uldale and Crooked Sike becks meet. A short distance from this meeting point there was an inscribed border stone known as Hollow Mill Cross which dated back at least to the 16th century. A local legend tells us that there, in 1664, a stocking buyer named John Smith returning to Kirkby Stephen with two ponies laden with knitted stockings and other garments, was foully murdered. Suspicion fell on a Westmorland farmer named James Hutchinson but there was not enough evidence to convict him.

The local story is that, two years later, Hutchinson was returning home in a thunderstorm after attending a funeral in Muker, and saw the ghost of his victim. He was greatly startled and his horse, already frightened by the storm, threw him

3. *The extraordinary stone pillars of Nine Standards Rigg.*

and dashed him to death against the stone cross. Like many legends, this story seems likely to be based on fact. There is little doubt that a murder took place though suspicion fell not only on Hutchinson but on James Alderson, a farmer from Thwaite, and other members of the Alderson family. However, a petition was raised in favour of these Aldersons and records show that it was signed by no less than thirty three other Aldersons, eighteen Milners, eleven Harkers and seven Metcalfs. Needless to say, nobody was ever found guilty of the murder.

In the year 1819, Birkdale is known to have had a population of forty-seven people but today it is a lonely largely uninhabited valley through which the road leads over to Kirkby Stephen. At the point where the Birkdale and Sleddale Becks begin leaving the amphitheatre, they join together and form the River Swale. Here at the junction of the two becks is the substantial old farmhouse known as Stone House, the origins of which go back to the 17th century. Local people recall that, at the peak of the mining era, there was a small chapel nearby. The building stone came from the nearby Hill Top quarry and George and Charles Alderson built two excellent stone bridges over the Swale a short distance below Stone House. These bridges were completed about 1840, and the stonework in both, as well in the walls nearby, is of the highest quality.

As it begins its journey to the Vale of York, the River reaches Hoggarths Bridge and on the hillside above the bridge is what remains of Hoggarths farm. It was built over 200 years ago at the foot of Great Ash Gill, on the lower slopes of Great Shunner Fell. Originally the home of the Hoggarth family, the farm was tenanted in 1899 by the Kilburn family. One day in July of that year there was a tremendous cloudburst over Shunner Fell and a great force of water swept down Great Ash Gill and poured through the farmhouse. Fortunately, the Kilburns were able to

4. *Stone House above which the Birkdale and Sleddale Becks
meet to form the River Swale.*

5. *One of the two fine Alderson bridges over the Swale
below Stone House.*

escape through an upstairs window but their home and most of their belongings were lost.

On reaching the River below, the force of the water swept away Hoggarths Bridge, an important crossing of the Swale. The bridge was later rebuilt a little way downstream and is in use today. Hoggarths house was also rebuilt but on the opposite side of the River and on a site well above the flooding level. Stone to rebuild the house came from the old homestead and from the nearby Little Moor Foot mine. Hoggarths is now the home of George Calvert and his family — George's grandmother was Mrs Kilburn who escaped with her husband William from the original house.

Though farming in Upper Swaledale during the 17th and 18th centuries could provide a basic if not prosperous existence, life for the local community was never easy and Hoggarths in the last century would have been no exception. In those times, the only alternative to farming for the young men of the Dale was to find work in the lead mines. By 1830, mining in Upper Swaledale had passed its peak. Mines were beginning to close, there was growing unemployment, increasing poverty and a feeling of despair amongst the mining community. It was then that many young Dalesmen realised that there was little future for them in Swaledale and they must seek a livelihood elsewhere. Some went to Lancashire to work in the cotton mills and others to the coal mines of Durham. But there were those, mainly the sons of the older Dale's families who decided to emigrate to the Middle West area of America. There, it was said, lead mining was starting to develop and there was both work and land available.

Amongst the Dalesmen who decided to cross the Atlantic was a son of the Waistell family who lived in the original Hoggarths Farm at the beginning of the last century. Thomas Waistell was born there in 1800, and, although by 1842 he was no longer a young man he decided that year to emigrate to

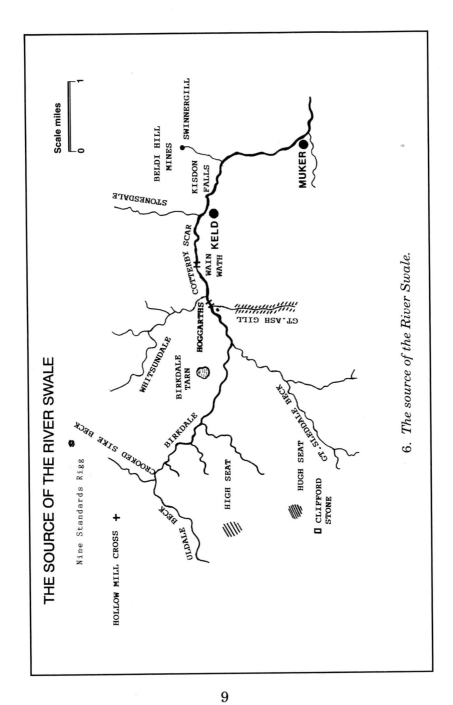

6. *The source of the River Swale.*

America. He found his way to Wisconsin where, like many other emigrant Swaledale men, he soon found work in the lead mines and gradually became well established in his new country. Records show that he lived until he was 87 years old and died in Schullsburg, Wisconsin where he had made his home. He is thought never to have returned to Swaledale.

CHAPTER II

The Arrival of the Norsemen, Keld, the Beldi Dispute and the Village of Muker

NO STUDY OF THE RIVER SWALE and its history would be complete without mention of the part played by the Norsemen invaders who arrived some eleven centuries ago. It was in the latter part of the ninth century that the North West coast of England was invaded by Norsemen who came via Ireland and the Isle of Man. They penetrated westwards and into the Lake District, some crossing the Pennines and reaching Upper Swaledale and Arkengarthdale. They found little habitation as the Anglians had not moved into the higher parts of these dales.

As the Norsemen were by tradition pastoral farmers they began to clear suitable areas where they could graze their cattle and sheep and build scattered farmsteads and longhouses. The invaders left their mark in many local place names and there are surnames in Swaledale,including Hoggarth and others such as Broderick and Heseltine, which are known to have Norse origins. Similarities can also exist between the Norwegian language and the Swaledale dialect still spoken by some of the older people of the Upper Dale.

As the Swale leaves Hoggarths Bridge it is joined by Whitsundale Beck which rises in the moorland watershed to the north and on its downward journey passes the farms of Raven Seat. The name is derived from the 'Hrafn Saetr' the place where the Norseman Hrafn established a pasture. Here there is an ancient packhorse bridge reminding us that Raven Seat was on the jagger route connecting with Kirkby Stephen, Tan Hill and Barnard Castle. In the early part of the 18th century there were at least seven families living in what was then 'the village' of Raven Seat, a sufficient number apparently to justify a small chapel and also a public house which probably gained additional trade from travellers on the jagger route.

Passing the steep cliffs of Cotterby Scar, the Swale reaches Wain Wath Force, one of the most picturesque falls in the area. The name has Norse origins and means a waggon crossing suggesting that the Norsemen must have used a ford above the falls. After being joined by Stonesdale Beck the River then flows over the rocky Catrake Falls and down to Keld, the highest village in Swaledale.

Keld was the site of a Norse settlement and the name can be related to the word 'Appeltekelda' meaning the spring near the apple tree. If we go back to 12,000 BC we learn that a glacier moving down Swaledale left a moraine above what is now Keld and this changed the course of the River. The site of the village may originally have been an island and there is evidence that the River then flowed down to the west of Kisdon Hill, passed the present village of Thwaite and then on to Muker. However, as a result of the moraine, the Swale forced a channel through the limestone strata making a new course between Kisdon and Beldi Hill on the way to Muker. This change of course is thought to have created the Catrake and the impressive Kisdon Falls.

At one time, Keld was a busy village standing at the head of Swaledale. It had a school, public house, a village hall, and shops. According to Leland there was a chapel at Keld in 1530 but history relates that, following a riot, it had to be closed.

This was probably because of disputes amongst the local inhabitants about the dissolution of the monasteries. Certainly, by 1789, it was in a ruinous state and was rebuilt only because of the efforts of a preacher named Edward Stillman. He walked all the way to London to raise £700 for the rebuilding, spending only sixpence during his travels and returning to Keld with the money he had collected. He remained as minister in Keld for forty-eight years. The chapel however had no burial ground. Today, the population of Keld has dwindled, there is still a chapel, but no school or public house and the quiet of the village is broken only by the walkers who pass through and stay at the local Youth Hostel.

The history of Upper Swaledale, if not much of the Dale, is closely linked with the mining of lead and, as the River Swale leaves the spectacular Kisdon Falls, it flows down past what was the once rich mining area of Beldi. This was the beginning of an extensive complex of mining concessions which ran through the hills embracing Gunnerside Gill, Old Gang and on to Arkengarthdale. Mining became a great industry in the Dale and between the 17th and 19th centuries, the population increased to a figure many times larger than it is today. There was work to be had and, even though conditions were very poor and earnings variable and intermittent, men came looking for mining work from nearby Wensleydale and Teesdale, from Derbyshire, Westmorland and even Cornwall.

On the slopes of Beldi Hill and surveying the valley of the Swale stands Crackpot Hall which was built as a deer stalking lodge. Until the beginning of the 18th century, red deer frequented the area which was then well forested but the deer and much of the forest gradually disappeared with the development of lead mining. The Hall then became a farmhouse and though it is now in ruins, it was lived in until fairly recent years.

In 1738 the Hall came into the ownership of Thomas Smith of Easby and he leased the Hall and land to Parkes and

7. Crackpot Hall.
(WITH ACKNOWLEDGEMENTS TO MR AND MRS KENNETH GUY)

Company, a mining concern mainly comprised of three brothers. They were to mine the land and pay a royalty on the lead ore they took out. But in 1767, Parkes sub-let some of the land to two local men Richard Metcalfe and John Scott and their partner Leonard Hartley. These three began to mine and struck a rich vein of lead which was highly valued.

Lord Pomfret who owned considerable land in the area, then claimed that the land being mined by Richard Metcalfe and his partners was his and that all dues for the mines should be paid to him. There followed lively scenes between the miners of the opposing sides and a long and expensive law suit. Judgement was finally given against Lord Pomfret and, though he appealed to the House of Lords three times in two years, his case was lost.

It was a remarkable law suit in that, though it related only to a small mining area in Swaledale, it went to the highest court in the Land. The case was heard before a famous judge of that time, Lord Mansfield, and it is apparent that, in no small measure, the final judgement was swayed by a remarkable speech by the Scotsman Alexander Wedderburn, acting for Thomas Smith. Alexander Wedderburn was at that time the Solicitor General and he later became Lord Chancellor. The considerable expense which Lord Pomfret incurred in this case caused him to become heavily in debt and he was later imprisoned in the Tower of London. So ended an episode long remembered in local lead mining history.

East of Beldi Hill is Swinnergill, a ravine at the foot of which are the remains of the Beldi smelt mill. High up in the ravine is a cavern some sixty yards long which came to be known as Swinnergill Kirk. History relates that it was used as a place of worship by the early Nonconformists at the time when they were prevented from meeting in public and when everyone was obliged to attend services at the established church. The Swinnergill cavern is still there today and remains a place of considerable interest.

The Norsemen who arrived in Upper Swaledale at the end of the ninth century were certainly not Christians though some were converted later. However, religion was to play an important part in the history of Swaledale. In the 6th century the Anglian Kingdom of Deira comprised most of the Yorkshire we know today and Deira was later to be merged with Bernicia to form Northumbria. It was when King Edwin of Deira married the Christian Princess Aethelberga of Kent in 625 A.D that Christianity was introduced to the area; the ways in which it survived and the story of the Christian Bishop Paulinus and the blessing of the River Swale are contained in a later chapter.

Following the Norman Conquest, there was a period of some four centuries during which the monastic houses had considerable Catholic influence over the lives of the ordinary Dales

15

people. In 1241, for instance, the monks of Rievaulx Abbey were granted all the pasture land in the Upper Swaledale area including Muker.

With the Dissolution and the Reformation the established church became Protestant and many people in Swaledale found this difficult to accept. Some took an active part in the Pilgrimage of Grace; others seemingly accepted the Protestant Church but remained secretly adherent to their earlier Catholic beliefs. Yet there was an important development in 1580 when an Anglican chapel-of-ease was built at Muker and this was welcomed for it avoided the previous necessity for burials to take place at the Grinton Church. Until then, funeral parties had to journey for many miles along the banks of the Swale using what became a recognised Corpse Way leading into Grinton.

8. *The village of Muker.*

The Swaledale Corpse Way started from Keld or above and probably followed what was originally an ancient way down to Grinton, generally keeping to the north, most sunny, side of the Dale. Apart from burial parties the route must have been used by packhorse traffic for the movement of stock and by the lead miners. The historian Dr T.D. Whitaker suggested that the Corpse Way journey from the top of the Dale would probably have taken two days and the burial parties would have spent a night at a place like Feetham where there is now the Punch Bowl Inn. They would have carried their dead not in coffins but in rude wicker baskets.

Muker Church, dedicated to St Mary, was licensed by the Bishop of Chester in 1580 and it was one of the few churches built in the reign of Queen Elizabeth I. At that time, the Church was still in an unsettled state because of the rival attitudes towards the Reformation. In 1900, restoration work at Muker revealed evidence of an earlier building and possibly an original tower of a different shape. It is suggested by E.R. Fawcett who has written the history of the Church, that a former building on the site may have been sacked or destroyed by the Scots raiders.

It is interesting that the two bells which hang in the Church tower today were cast in the 13th century long before the dedication of the present building. Consequently their origin presents something of a mystery and they may not have come from the same source. It seems most probable however that they came from a local monastery after the Dissolution. Ellerton Priory is a likely source but there are no records to confirm this and the bells may have come from further afield.

The origin of Muker's rare communion cup is well recorded however; it came from the Goldsmiths of York and was made by George Kytchyng, a Freeman and goldsmith of the City. According to T.P. Cooper the York cyclic date-letter implies that the cup left the workshop of the silversmith in York in 1583.

17

9. *One of the two Muker Church bells.*
(BY PERMISSION OF THE REVEREND PETER MIDWOOD)

The name Muker can be interpreted as a small cultivated pasture and the history of the village certainly goes back to the Norsemen settlers and probably earlier. According to the late local historian Edmund Cooper, evidence has been found of bronze and iron age settlements in the area. The incoming Norsemen settled into farming and it is evident that some remained in Upper Swaledale for generations ultimately inter-marrying with Anglians.

By the 17th and 18th centuries, the great development in lead mining in the area brought a considerable growth in the population. Accommodation for the incoming miners was very limited with the result that people had to live in cramped conditions often with large families and their lodgers packed into small cottages. At the peak of the lead mining era, Muker and Gunnerside were the two main centres of population. There were three public houses in Muker, the Church and later a chapel, shops and a small smithy. In 1678, a school was endowed and in more recent times, its pupils included the well known naturalists Richard and Cherry Kearton.

Though lead mining developed into a major industry in the Dale, the conditions underground were extremely hard. To reach their work, miners frequently had to walk long distances and their average life span was below 50 years. Although the owners, investors and officials were often well rewarded, it was

18

nevertheless a precarious industry for the ordinary mining folk and as has been said, their earnings could be intermittent and variable. Unless they had access to a smallholding, many found it difficult to keep above the poverty level. Nearly every family relied on the extra money they could earn by knitting stockings and hats and, in the Muker area as in other parts of Upper Swaledale, hand knitting was an industry second only to lead mining.

When cheaper lead came to be imported from Spain in the 1820s, it became clear that the economy of Upper Swaledale could no longer provide for the size of the population. By the middle of the 19th century, many mining families without work and near poverty had already moved to the mills of Lancashire or to coal mining. By 1830, some of those who decided to emigrate began leaving their villages. Groups of young men, sad but full of hope for a future in the New World, had sold all but their basic belongings to raise money for the voyage across the Atlantic. The majority had never been out of the Dales and had never seen the sea, yet most of them were eventually to reach the American Middle West and settled well in their new country.

One of the earliest of the Dales emigrants was a lone young miner, John Harker[1], who left Muker in 1825, but his destination was the goldfields of Colombia in South America where he settled and made good. Though he died at the early age of 38 it was not before he had married and been given the high position of Superintendent of Mines. His descendants are still living in Colombia today.

Muker now has only a small population and the school has closed. Yet it retains an air of independence and is much favoured by the tourists. It has its own annual show and is still the centre of hand knitting in the Dale. The village continues to take great pride in the Muker Silver Band which is held in wide respect and has a history going back over more than ninety years.

CHAPTER III

Gunnerside and the Journey to Paradise

LEAVING MUKER AND FOLLOWING the course of the River, the Corpse Way passes Satron on its way to Grinton. Here at Satron there was one of the earliest corn mills in Upper Swaledale, and there is still a beautiful arched bridge spanning the River. It was built 300 years ago as a result of a legacy of £5 from Phillip Swale, a Quaker who had been Lord Wharton's Agent and a man of some wealth and influence, Near to the bridge is a 'coffin' stone used by corpse bearers resting during their journey down to Grinton.

10. Satron (Ivelet) Bridge.

Although the bridge at Satron (Ivelet) was not actually on a packhorse route, it clearly provided a link between manorial estates and connected with the Corpse Way route which was available for normal packhorse traffic. For over six centuries packhorses and mules were the main form of transport in the Dales carrying lead, woollens, household supplies and produce for the markets. Any bridges on the routes were designed to allow for passage of the laden packhorses.

A short distance downstream is Gunnerside, the Norse name for which was 'Gunnarr Saetr', meaning Gunnarr's seat, Gunnarr having been the Norse Chief who settled there. Gunnerside, perhaps even more than Muker, was very much at the centre of the great lead mining era. In Gunnerside Gill which rises steeply above the village, there was a great deal of mining activity. A major level — or underground horizontal tunnel — was started as late as 1864 in the lower section of the Gill and was named the Sir Francis level after Sir Francis Denys, son of the proprietor. There proved to be too many problems and it was thirteen years later before a rich vein of lead was revealed — the Friarfold Vein — whereupon there was great rejoicing amongst the miners. The remains of two dressing floors built to deal with the ore are still visible today.

In the upper part of the Gill was a concentration of earlier mines most of which were driven into the hillside after extensive hushing. The process of hushing used large quantities of water which washed away soil and loose rock, revealing the mineralised veins from which the ore could be extracted. It was an effective process though it permanently defaced much of the landscape of the Gill. Some of these earlier mines were given girls names like Priscilla, Dolly and Barbara and they worked into the complex system of mining operations leading to the famous Old Gang mines and on into Arkengarthdale. At the top of Gunnerside Gill were the Blakethwaite dam, levels and smelt mill the remains of which still provide interest for mining historians.

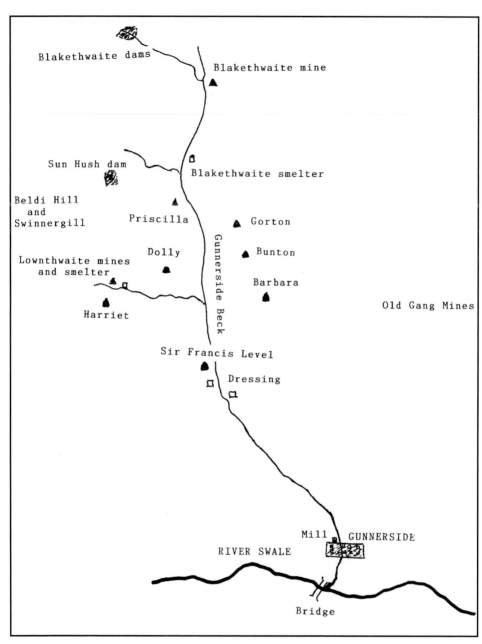

Blakethwaite dams

Blakethwaite mine

Sun Hush dam

Blakethwaite smelter

Beldi Hill
and
Swinnergill

Priscilla

Gorton

Dolly

Bunton

Lownthwaite mines
and smelter

Gunnerside Beck

Barbara

Harriet

Old Gang Mines

Sir Francis Level

Dressing

Mill   GUNNERSIDE

RIVER SWALE

Bridge

11. *Gunnerside Gill Mining Area.*

22

After the passing of the Toleration Act of 1689 the mining families, and others, were no longer obliged to follow one established religion. The Church of England had never won the hearts of many Dales folk and, apart from the Catholics who remained members of an underground church, many came to favour the Congregationalists and Presbyterians who had the support of Lord Philip Wharton and had several chapels including one at Smarber above Low Row.

Lord Wharton owned the Manor of Muker and half the Manor of Healaugh. Though he was regarded by his tenants as a hard landlord, he was fair and a man with strong religious feelings. He is often remembered for his Bible Charity which caused free bibles and catechisms to be distributed to poor children living on his estates.

Apart from support for the Congregationalists and Presbyterians, religious freedom brought some following for the Baptists and Quakers. For many mining families however, a new allegiance was to come with the development of Methodism. It was in the middle of the 18th century that the seeds of Methodism began to develop at Gunnerside and at Low Row, a few miles further down the Dale, a preaching room was set up and Jacob Rowell, a preacher appointed by John Wesley, became a familiar figure in the area.

In 1761 and again some years later, John Wesley himself came and preached to large gatherings. A chapel was built in Gunnerside in 1789 and by the end of the century Methodism had gained a great following amongst the mining community. It is interesting that, when the lead mining industry in the Dale went into recession and numbers of families emigrated to the Mississippi area of America, they continued to follow their Methodist faith and built several chapels in the lead mining areas where they settled.

Gunnerside once had an inn called the Miners Arms and there was a corn[2] mill latterly known as Percivals Mill. Having earlier been worked by the Milner family, it was taken over by James Percival when he came into Swaledale with his family from Wensleydale in the first half of the 19th century. His mill was sited on the west side of the fast running Gunnerside beck which provided water to power the mill. The beck rises some three or four miles up in the hills between Rogans Seat and Water Crag which is at the centre of the lead mining area and its waters fall down the slopes of Gunnerside Gill to join the Swale below Gunnerside Bridge. Like most other becks in the Dale it is liable to flood very quickly after any heavy rain, and the flood water pours into the River Swale. Not for the first time, Gunnerside Bridge was washed away by flood waters in 1890 and had to be rebuilt.

Over the years, the tendency of the Swale to rise very quickly and to develop great power as it swept down the Dale not only destroyed several bridges but it resulted in a number of local people being drowned. It has been said that more people were drowned in the Swale during the lead mining era than were killed in mining accidents. Most drowning deaths resulted from trying to ford across the Swale when the water was rising. It seems likely that few Dales people knew how to swim and this was probably the reason why, for example, a local man, George Blades, was drowned at the Satron Corn Mill in 1650 and John Harker, a Muker Sunday School teacher, was drowned in the Swale in 1850.

Below Gunnerside Bridge are the Isles and Low Whita Bridges both of which have had to be rebuilt after destructive flooding of the River. Isles Bridge was originally built in wood about 1734 and in 1801, after it had been washed away, a local yeoman farmer Richard Garth canvassed the people for money to build a new bridge. When a new stone bridge was erected it was badly damaged by a further major flood in 1883 and the arches had to be rebuilt.

High on the hill above the Swale as it flows down to Isles Bridge is Summer Lodge Tarn, a great haunt for black headed gulls in the breeding season. From the Tarn a beck flows down into what is known as Bloody Vale. Legend tells us that, following the Battle of Bannockburn in 1314, there was a battle here between local men and a group of Scottish raiders whose leader known as 'the laird' was killed in the action along with the other raiders. The remains of armour and some axes were reported to have been found in the vicinity early last century. Below Bloody Vale the waters of the beck fall steeply down Crackpot Gill and join the main River, passing on the way the site of a former landmark, Haverdale Mill.

The name Haverdale comes from the Norse word 'halfri' meaning oats, confirming that in earlier times crops of oats were regularly grown in this area of Swaledale. Haverdale was originally built as a worsted mill for making carpets probably on the site of an earlier corn mill and using water power from the beck. It was owned by the well known local family of Knowles who, by 1853, established themselves as worsted spinners and hosiery manufacturers.

The build up of this family business has been largely attributed to Edmund Knowles. As well as being involved in the knitting and weaving trades he was was variously described as an innkeeper, farmer, hosier, and lessee of coal and lead mines. Certainly he seems to have been a man of many parts but clearly a driving force in all he undertook. Haverdale Mill thrived for many years making carpets and blankets but when new machinery was installed the local Haverdale beck could not provide the necessary force of water and eventually the mill had to close. For a time it came to be used as a corn mill but this also failed and as the years passed the Haverdale building became a ruin.

Across Isles Bridge to the north side of the river and standing below the village of Low Row is an impressive house known as Paradise. It was built in 1653 by the Fryer family and long before water-powered machines were available, hand-powered devices were installed there for preparing and spinning wool, mainly for knitting. This equipment was installed by the Fryer family, continued by another family — the Parkes — and then taken over by the Knowles.

The Knowles are known to have employed a group of full time knitters who worked in a large top storey room in Paradise with other staff, a hose dresser, wool carder, three spinners, warehousemen and clerks. They produced yarn for the Haverdale carpets, knitted stockings and seamen's jerseys. The Knowles family business had historic significance not only because the family lived in Paradise where the woollens were produced but because their business was a rare survivor in the transitional period between people working in their own homes and being employed in a factory. By the mid-19th century however, the century of steam had arrived, hand knitting and hand-loom weaving were no longer commercially viable, and the Knowles business closed down.

12. *Paradise – once a centre for wool spinning and knitting.*

Low Whita Bridge, Scabba Wath, The Early History of Harkerside and Calva Hill, Reeth and the Swales of Grinton

As THE SWALE CONTINUES ITS journey down the Dale from Isles Bridge it passes Low Houses, a group of 18th century buildings including the attractive Lawn House built in 1766 at a

13. Lawn House – built in the 18th century at a time when the mine owners were reaping the benefit of a developing lead mining industry.

14. *James L. Broderick – a land agent and member of an old Swaledale farming family. His diary revealed much about life in the Dale in the 19th century and of his journey to America in 1876.*
(BY PERMISSION OF LOREN N. HORTON, IOWA STATE HISTORICAL DEPARTMENT)

time when mine owners were reaping the benefits of a developing lead mining industry. The house is built close to the river bank and in more recent times it was here that Thomas Armstrong, author of 'The Crowthers of Bankdam' and 'Adam Brunskill' made his home. Nearby is a Dales farmhouse occupied by the Harker family for many years. James Harker lived there in 1840 and had his initials and the date carved above the doorway. Another Harker homestead for many years was Spring End Farmhouse above Gunnerside,where Simon Harker had his initials carved by the doorway in 1790. Indeed, over the centuries, Harker became a dominant name in parts of Upper Swaledale. Reeth Parish Council records indicate that, as early as 1674, there were seven Harkers living in the area, whilst in the parish of Muker and Melbecks there were no less than twelve families of this name.

Spring End was also the home of one of the oldest yeoman families of Upper Swaledale, the Brodericks. The diaries of two members of the family, Edward and James, provided a unique record of 19th century life in Swaledale and James gave an important account of the experiences of the Dales men and women who emigrated to America. Others in the Broderick family are known to have had very independent opinions and two are buried on a hill above Spring End, rather than in a local churchyard.

Across the River from Low Houses is Feetham with its early 17th century Punch Bowl Inn which in the lead mining days was known as the Miners Arms. This was partly burnt down in 1929 but was rebuilt in its original form. The Low Whita Bridge — also known as Scabba Wath Bridge — crosses the River between Feetham and Healaugh. Scabba Wath was the name given to an ancient foot-ford believed to be used by Roman soldiers travelling from their camp at Bainbridge in Wensleydale to their permanent fort at Greta Bridge on the important trans-Pennine route from Scotch Corner to Carlisle. From Scabba Wath their route is thought to have taken them

15. *Low Whita Bridge.*

16. *Healaugh village and Calva Hill where, together with Harkerside, important excavation work has been carried out as part of the Swaledale Ancient Boundaries project.*

to Feetham and west of Calva Hill to Arkengarthdale and over the Stang to Barnard Castle, a similar route followed by the road today.

The extensive hillside sloping to the south of the Swale was given the name Harkerside. The Norse word 'akr' means an acre or open field and, as it was Scandinavian custom to appropriate a place name for a family, historians conclude that 'akr' became Arkar and eventually Harker. Oatmeal being a staple food in these early times, there seems no doubt that Harkerside was a cultivated area with oats being the main crop. In recent years, the area of Harkerside and of Calva on the north side of the Swale have been subjected to an intensive survey by the Swaledale Ancient Boundaries Project. This work has resulted in the mapping of wide ranging organised systems of prehistoric land divisions using a combination of intensive fieldwork and aerial photography. The project has also carried out research into early occupation of this part of Swaledale by examination of the pollen record in deep peat deposits and of plant remains in soil samples.

Evidence has been found of coaxial field systems, major boundaries which follow one prevailing axis, and platforms on which the early inhabitants used to build their houses, usually inside walled enclosures. Of necessity, these platforms were often scooped or terraced into the hillside. A short distance above Healaugh for instance, a group of six or seven house-platforms was located enclosed within a bank or wall to form a settlement enclosure with an entrance on the downhill side. The area also includes evidence of other house-platforms some of which were not enclosed. Across the Swale on Harkerside were found traces of extensive settlements covering much of the hillside. Here also is Maiden Castle the name of which seems to be derived from the celtic 'mai-dun', meaning a ridge. This was an embanked settlement and is likely to be of late bronze or iron age origin. It may well have been used for a time as the headquarters of the extensive Harkerside settlements.

The research work carried out in this area of Swaledale has been considerable and, in his description of 'Early Land Division and Settlement in Swaledale', T.C. Laurie refers to the dramatic location of two high level field systems on the side of Fremington Edge above Reeth and facing across to Calva hill. The airy and elevated position chosen for these settlements with their roundhouse foundations clearly had no regard for shelter bearing in mind the very exposed position of the Fremington Edge escarpment which is 1,500 feet high (457m).

Research has indeed brought to light rich archaeological remains and ancient settlement sites which were virtually unknown until recently. Thanks to the dedicated work of those concerned with this research, there is now clear evidence of iron and bronze age as well as Romano-British habitation on

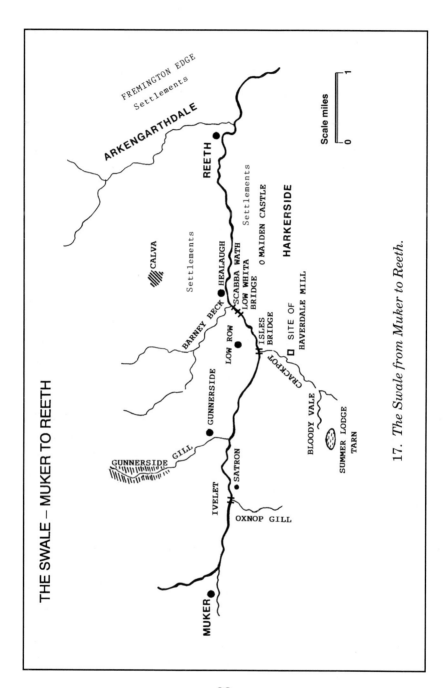

THE SWALE – MUKER TO REETH

17. *The Swale from Muker to Reeth.*

a scale not previously appreciated, the period of this habitation being between 2000 B.C. and 30 A.D. Traces of much earlier, mesolithic, hunting camps have also been located.

When the Norsemen invaders settled in Swaledale towards the end of the 9th century, they limited their occupation to the upper part of the Dale. They probably advanced little further than Gunnerside where they are known to have built a 'longhouse' though they must have reached Feetham, adjacent to Low Row, as the name is derived from the Norse word 'Fitjum', meaning a meadow.

Though these Norsemen seemed content to remain in the upper part of the Dale, the Angles certainly reached Healaugh the name of which is derived from the Anglian word ' Helagh' (or 'Helah') which can be interpreted as a stronghold in a forest clearing. After the Norman settlement, it became an important centre as head of the very extensive Manor of Healaugh, an area of some 40,000 acres and, standing as it did in the centre of a well stocked forest, it was soon a favoured centre for hunting. Walter de Gaunt, who died in 1138, and his wife Matilda built a hunting lodge close to Healaugh village and history relates that the famous John of Gaunt visited Healaugh on several occasions. In later years, following a division of the Manor lands, Sir Francis Bigod lived there as a landowner until his execution at the time of the Pilgrimage of Grace. After the Dissolution, Healaugh became part of the extensive estate of Thomas, the first Lord Wharton.

After the Norman settlement, Anglian Reeth was for a long time much less important than Healaugh. Reported as being only waste land in the Domesday Survey, its subsequent recovery was very slow. It suffered, as many villages did, not only from the Scottish raids, but also from a succession of very bad farming years and the consequences of the Black Death. Not until 1695 had it developed enough to hold a weekly market and have an annual fair. It had a mill which was sited by the

Arkle, a tributary of the Swale. The Arkle Beck rises on the very edge of Stainmore Forest just seven kilometres from the old Roman road and the Rey Cross Roman camp. Indeed, during the Roman period and probably in prehistoric times, the Arkle provided an access route from the Swale valley to the Stainmore Pass and the ancient and important trans- Pennine crossing which is now the A66.

Like others in the Dale, particularly during the 18th and early 19th centuries, the villagers of Reeth depended a great deal on any money they could earn hand knitting stockings. Reeth benefited however from its location at the junction of Arkengarthdale with Swaledale, and began to gain importance more as a commercial and farming centre than a mining village. Today it is the largest village in Swaledale and a centre for the local commercial and tourist trades.

As the Swale approaches Grinton, it passes Swale Hall which dates back at least to the late 16th century. When Walter de Gaunt, who was a kinsman of William the Conqueror, married Matilda the daughter of the Breton Earl of Richmond she was given 'the whole of Swaledale' by her father as a dowry. Walter then became the first Lord of Swaledale and he and his wife gave the church and Manor of Grinton to Bridlington Priory, retaining the extensive Manor of Healaugh.

Walter subsequently granted the Manor of West Grinton to his nephew Alured who apparently adopted the surname Swale after the name of the River. He and his descendants remained in possession of the family home Swale House until the reign of Queen Anne. Perhaps the most eminent of these descendants was Solomon Swale, a barrister who was made Member of Parliament for Aldborough, near Boroughbridge and was created a baronet in 1660. He was buried at St Martins-in-the-Fields in London. Misfortune overtook the family when his grandson Sir Solomon Swale, the third baronet, became involved in several law suits concerning his failure to renew the lease of the chief part of the Swale estate then held by the Crown. As a result of this omission the family was obliged to relinquish Swale Hall which was sold by auction. Sadly, Sir Solomon finished his days in a debtors prison and died in 1733, a ruined and broken hearted man.

In the north chancel of Grinton's St Andrew's Church is the memorial stone of the Swale family of Swale Hall. This is an old church affectionately known by many as the cathedral of the Dale. Its history goes back to Norman times though much of the building including the nave and the chancel are 15th century. In 1762, the Vicarage was known to be a short distance away in what is now the Grinton Post Office. Over the doorway, is the inscription T.D. being the initials of the Reverend Timothy Dickinson, Vicar from 1742-83. As already mentioned, until a church was built at Muker, all burials had to be conducted at Grinton which meant a long journey for mourners to bring their dead down from Upper Swaledale.

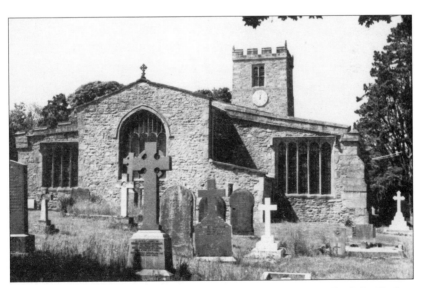

18. *Grinton Church, often referred to as the cathedral of the Dale.*

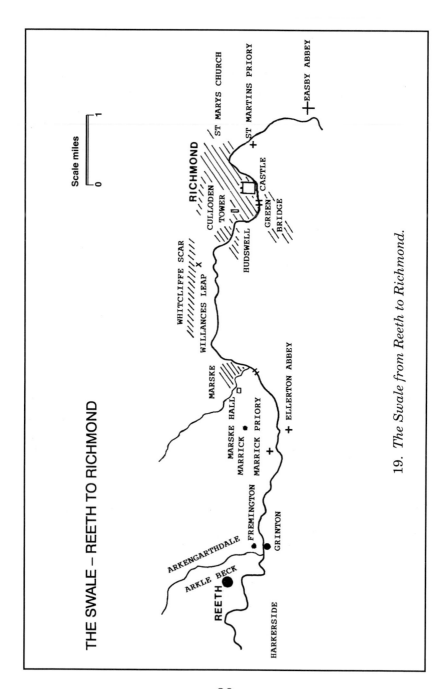

19. *The Swale from Reeth to Richmond.*

Grinton Bridge over the Swale was built in the middle of the 16th century and later widened to the design of John Carr of York. Immediately adjoining the Bridge is the impressive Blackburn Hall which bears the date 1665 and the initials of Elizabeth Hutton Blackburn, the niece of Sir Timothy Hutton of Marske Hall, a member of an important Dales family to which reference is made in a later chapter.

On the north side of the Bridge is the village of Fremington. This is a name probably derived from the Saxon 'Fremd' interpreted as 'the place of strangers' and it is thought to have been a settlement of Anglo-Celtic people. There is evidence of an ancient dyke or entrenchment crossing the valley at Fremington and pursuing a direction parallel with the earthworks on Harkerside. The date of this is uncertain but it appears to have been a substantial defensive barrier possibly connected with the Scots Dyke at Richmond.

Since the eighteenth century, the dominant building in Fremington has been Draycott Hall, previously known as Fremington Hall. The name was changed to Draycott to commemorate Anna Maria Draycott, Countess of Pomfret who inherited the royalties from the mines in the Manors of Healaugh and Muker from the family of the Dukes of Wharton. In 1963 the Draycott Hall manuscripts were released and made available for historical research. They contain details of leases, plans and correspondence dated back to 1779 and provide an important and fascinating insight into the Swaledale lead mining industry at its peak.

CHAPTER V

Marrick and Ellerton Priories – The Hutton Family of Marske

As THE RIVER SWALE LEAVES Grinton, it passes to the south the imposing late 18th century Cogden Hall built for the lord of the manor of East Grinton, John Readshaw, probably on the site of an earlier fortified building. John Readshaw was the son of Caleb Readshaw described in his time[3] as an 'opulent and eminent Richmond merchant' who was involved in the stocking knitting trade, brickbuilding and lead mining. However, Caleb became indebted to Sir Thomas Dundas of Aske Hall and in 1790 he was made bankrupt.

After leaving Grinton Bridge. the River flows through some pleasant meadowland before reaching the ancient Priory of Marrick. This is on the north side of the River and was founded by Roger de Aske for the Benedictine nuns about 1150. It was well endowed with land, grazing rights and other property and was given the Marrick Church of St Andrew. Administration was the responsibility of the Prioress who was called upon to apply the Benedictine rules strictly but with fairness, yet there were limits to her authority. A Master was appointed to control the management of the Priory's estates and the Archbishop was always able to assert his powers of direction. Amongst the Benedictine houses, as well as the Cistercians and Gilbertines, there was well founded concern in the 13th century and later to prevent any move towards worldly materialism.

Monastic land however could be used to produce wealth, more especially through the sale of wool. Some of the larger monastic houses in particular found that wool trading in the commercial world provided a highly lucrative source of income. The Cistercians of Fountains Abbey, for instance, found difficulty in reconciling the wealth of their wool trade with their monastic vows. Records produced in 1315 showed that the nuns at Marrick had sufficient grazing rights to provide an annual average of eight sacks of wool, equivalent to some 3,024 lbs. This was very small compared with Fountains Abbey's seventy six sacks but it would have provided some valued income for the Priory.

H.F.M. Prescott's 'The Man on the Donkey' gives an impression of a relaxed rather than severe way of life at Marrick Priory in the period prior to the Dissolution. It is known that the nuns were allowed to employ as many secular women as were required for work regarded as unbecoming for the nuns to undertake themselves and it is evident that lay sisters and lay brethren participated in some of the religious activities. Marrick had the distinction of being allowed to exist for several years after the Dissolution and records show that at the time of its surrender to the Crown in November 1540 there was a Prioress and sixteen nuns.

Today, the Priory buildings which remain are used to provide a Christian centre of activity, mainly for young people. The village of Marrick stands high above the Priory and the River and, in the days of the nunnery, access to the village was up a stone 'causey' comprised of 365 steps through the wooded hillside. This route from the Priory can still be used though many of the steps have disappeared.

A short distance from Marrick Priory but on the opposite bank of the River are the remains of the Ellerton Priory, a small establishment of white clothed Cistercian nuns. Its origins seem obscure but it has been referred to as one of the most

20. *Ellerton Abbey.*

humble and the poorest of monastic foundations. Ellerton had some grazing rights but little property and apparently only limited income from wool sales. It had the misfortune to suffer from the Scottish raids into Swaledale. The Scots entered the Priory and took away charters and writings. At the Dissolution there were only five nuns at Ellerton. Little now remains except the Priory tower which is 15th century and stands in a field above the River bank.

Until nearly the end of the 17th century no road crossed the Swale between Grinton and Richmond but John Hutton of Marske asked permission of the Sessions to make a bridge across the Swale 'betwixt Dounham and Maske' and said he would pay part of the cost. A bridge was indeed built in 1674 and it was in a beautiful setting three miles downstream from Ellerton. Like others however, Downholme bridge suffered from a great flood in 1771 but it was rebuilt two years later under the supervision of the famous John Carr, Bridgemaster for the North Riding.

At the nearby village of Downholme, sited to the south of the River, is the quaint late 12th century Church of St Michael and All Angels and a little further away is Walburn Hall, a fine Elizabethan fortified manor house once the home of the Sedgewick and later the Lascelles families. The principal rooms were on the first floor and the ground floor was given over to servants quarters, kitchens and the farm. The Hall was garrisoned against the king during the Civil War and, early in the 17th century, the Lascelles family were forced to sell their estates mainly because of recusancy fines. The building was restored by the Hutton family in the 19th century.

Across Downholme Bridge it is a short distance to the village of Marske, the name of which is derived from the Anglo-Saxon word 'merse' meaning a marsh or hollow. The manor of Marske is believed to have been held originally by the family of De Merse but, by the end of the 16th century the family of Huttons had begun an association with Marske which was to last over three hundred years. It was a remarkable family producing two archbishops, both having the name Matthew Hutton, two High Sheriffs and a Member of Parliament. The names Matthew, Timothy and John are repeated down the Hutton family tree over the many generations and the records show that there were several marriages with members of other important local families such as the Bowes, the Darcys and the Stapyltons.

Matthew I was the founder of this great family. He entered Pembroke College, Cambridge in 1546 and later became a Fellow of his College. He was made Regius Professor of Divinity in 1561 and was elected Vice-Chancellor in his early thirties. Matthew attracted the attention of Queen Elizabeth I when she visited Cambridge and in 1567 he was advanced to the Deanery of York and in 1589 he became Bishop of Durham in what was a difficult period for the Church. Finally. he was elevated to be Archbishop of York and on his death in 1606 he was buried in York Minster.

It was at the instigation of Archbishop Matthew that, in 1601, the Manor of Marske was conveyed to his eldest son Timothy who married the daughter of Sir George Bowes of Streatlam Castle, in County Durham. Timothy received a knighthood in 1605, he was an Alderman of Richmond and High

Sheriff of Yorkshire. Having acquired the Marske estate he began rebuilding Marske Hall. Generations of Huttons are recorded as having had large families. Timothy and his wife produced thirteen children and, of those who survived, it was their son Matthew II who continued the family line after marrying Barbara, a daughter of Sir Conyers Darcy.

One of their seven children was John who married into the Stapylton family of Myton (see chapter 16). He and his wife produced another John, a grandson for Matthew II, and he was to become Member of Parliament for Richmond during the years 1701-2. He also held a position with the interesting description of 'Bowbearer in the new forest of Arkilgarthdale'. When this John married, he and his wife continued the family line and one of their children, given the family name of Matthew, became Archbishop of Canterbury. He was born at Marske and attended school at Ravensworth near Richmond, then becoming Bishop of Bangor in 1743 and four years later Archbishop of York. In 1757 he was enthroned Primate of all England.

21. Marske Hall, the home of the Hutton family.

Archbishop Matthew had a brother — yet another John — who held the rank of Captain and is credited with raising a company of foot-soldiers for the suppression of the 1745 rebellion. Apart from constructing new stables, he did much to improve the building of Marske Hall. Further down the family line, it was his grandson, also given the name John, who attained the position of High Sheriff of Yorkshire as had his ancestor Timothy in 1605.

Today, high on the hill above Marske and the Swale stands an obelisk erected in 1814 as a memorial to the burial place of John's younger brother Matthew Hutton of Macclesfield who died in 1814 aged 35 years. The obelisk is referred to locally as the Hutton Memorial perhaps with the wish that it should embrace the memory of all members of this great family.

CHAPTER VI

The Norman Castle and the Historic Buildings of Richmond

As the River approaches Richmond it passes the cliffs of Whitcliffe Scar. It was here in 1606 that Robert Willance, an Alderman and wealthy local draper, rode into thick fog whilst hunting and galloped his horse over the edge of the cliff. The fall of two hundred feet killed the horse but Robert Willance escaped with a broken leg. He managed to keep alive until help arrived by cutting open the horse and laying his leg against the warm flesh. At the top of the cliff there are monuments commemorating his escape from death. Below Whitcliffe Scar there is the site of an ancient encampment reported to date as early as 4000 BC. and there are traces of a main dwelling area and a moat which encircled the site.

Without doubt, the dominant feature of Richmond is the Norman Castle and, from the River Swale, its south walls seem quite impenetrable. Occupying a strategic site in a command-ing position high above the River, the Castle was built by Earl Alan who fought at the Battle of Hastings and was one of William the Conqueror's most trusted supporters. As a reward for his services, Alan had been given a huge area of land and Swaledale was included in his Yorkshire estates. From the stronghold of the Castle his garrison could dominate Swaledale and the surrounding countryside and — as the King intended

— keep the peasantry in order and deter any invasion from the north.

The building of the Castle began in 1071 and, unlike the motte-and-bailey castles of that time, it was built of stone. The Keep which towers over the town was completed a century later. Until the middle ages the Castle continued to be used both as a fortress, prison and residence. Though it was never attacked, the invading Scots penetrated as far as Richmond early in the 14th century and had to be 'bought off'[4] by payment of substantial sums of money.

The Castle was frequently used for housing prisoners during the 12th and 13th centuries and retained a political significance until the 16th century. By then however it was beginning to suffer from decay and when Leland visited it in the 16th century, he referred to it as a 'mere ruin'. However, it was never wholly neglected and some repair work was completed in the 18th and 19th centuries. In the First World War, it was used as a depot of the Non-Combatant Corps, formed for men conscripted into the army who had conscientious objection to bearing arms. Today, the Keep and the remaining walls of the Castle are well maintained and attract many visitors.

The town of Richmond grew up under the protection of the Castle and consisted mainly of burgages grouped round a central market place which was originally the Castle's outer bailey. The Chapel of Holy Trinity was founded in the outer bailey in 1150 and, though it had no burial ground, it was apparently intended to serve both the Castle garrison and the local people. Shortly after the Chapel's foundation however, the Church of St Mary was built a short distance from the Town centre and it provided a much needed burial area. The Trinity Chapel building with its tower then came to be used at various times as a court, warehouse, cellarage, a school and a prison as well as a chapel. The main part of the building now houses the Green Howards museum and only a small Holy Trinity chapel remains which is still used for worship.

45

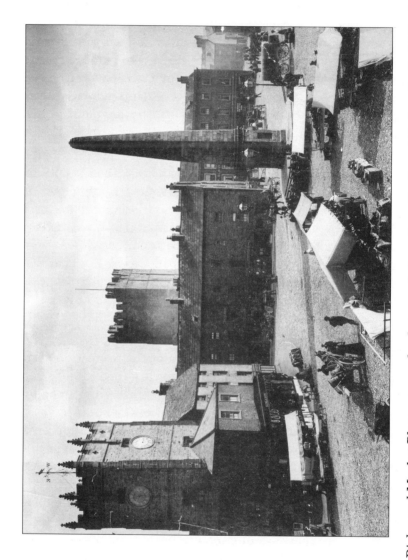

22. *Richmond Market Place – an early photograph from the collection of the late Leslie P. Wenham.*

The new Church dedicated to St Mary was built on the hillside east of the Castle and overlooking the River Swale below. The date of its foundation is not known but the Church was confirmed to the Monastery of St Mary in York in 1147. It has a fine early-15th century west tower but externally the Church today is mostly the work of Sir George Gilbert Scott who restored it in 1859-60. Though the interior is a little disappointing there is a 15th century font and some magnificent choir stalls[5] in the chancel which originated from Easby Abbey and were made shortly before the Abbey's 1536 Dissolution. The Church also possesses a 'mouseman' pulpit and several other items of furniture by Thompson of Kilburn. On the chancel south wall is an imposing monument to Sir Timothy Hutton. Both Sir Timothy and his wife are buried below this monument on which they are depicted kneeling towards the east above the small figures of eight surviving children and four swaddled babies each with a coat of arms and an inscription.

In 1313, a murage grant allowed for the building of a Richmond town wall intended primarily as a protection against Scottish raids. The wall had two main gates and two postern gates one at Cornforth Hill and the other at Fryers Wynd giving access to the Franciscan Friary.Though Leland thought that the walls in the 16th century were in a ruinous state, sections are still preserved today particularly in the area of the two postern gates.

The Friary was founded in 1258 to the north of the market place and it remained a comparatively simple structure until the late 15th century when the tower was built. At the time of the Friary's dissolution in 1539 there was a warden and fourteen brethren and it is evident that for nearly three centuries the Grey Friars had played a leading role in the religious life of Richmond. Today, the well preserved Friary Tower provides the most attractive example of medieval architecture in Richmond.

There are many other interesting buildings in this historic town. The 12th century Chapel of St Edmund the King for instance is sited on the east side of Richmond in the area known as Anchorage Hill. In 1607, this became the Eleanor Bowes hospital, an alms house for widows. On the road out of Richmond to Brompton on Swale is St Nicholas which was founded in the 12th century as a hospital, re-founded by Queen Mary and finally dissolved by Queen Elizabeth I. In the Civil War it became the headquarters of the Scottish army and in 1813 it was tastefully restored by Ignatius Bonomi. A later building of importance to Richmond is the Georgian Theatre Royal. Built in 1788 by actor-manager Samuel Butler, the Theatre closed after about a century of seasons and was used as a warehouse. However it re-opened as a living theatre in 1962 and it continues to play an active part in Richmond life. No other contemporary theatre survives in such a complete state.

On the Riverside close to the area known as The Green there was a 17th century mansion known as Yorke House which was demolished in 1823. It was the home of the Yorkes, an important local family several of whom served as Richmond members of Parliament. One of their number, John Yorke, is credited with building a remarkable octagonal tower on the hillside above Yorke House. It was originally called the Cumberland Temple and was intended to celebrate the victory of the Duke of Cumberland's army over Prince Charles Edward Stuart the Jacobite Young Pretender at the Battle of Culloden near Inverness. The Culloden Tower as it is called today, was built on the site of a pele tower known as Hudswell Tower which stood there between the 14th and 15th centuries.

The earliest and historically the most important bridge over the Swale at Richmond is generally known as the Green Bridge[6] which crosses the River below the massive and dominant walls of the Castle. The original Green Bridge is

known to have been in existence in about 1535 when John
Leland, King's Antiquary to
Henry VIII, visited the town.
The boundary between the
Borough of Richmond and the
North Riding of Yorkshire ran
along the middle of the Swale
at this point and Richmond
claimed the right to levy tolls
on all goods using the bridge.
By the middle of the 18th century, the Bridge was in a poor
state and needing repair.
Responsibility for its maintenance was shared between
Richmond Corporation and
the North Riding of Yorkshire
but there was no co-ordination

23. *The Culloden Tower.*

between the two and they each carried out repairs to their portion of the structure when they deemed it necessary.

In the autumn of 1771 a very severe flood damaged or
washed away several bridges over the Swale and, though
Richmond's Green Bridge survived, it needed constant attention. Ultimately, the North Riding decided that the Bridge had
to be taken down and rebuilt. Richmond Corporation prevari-
cated and only agreed when the North Riding threatened an
indictment. Yet both authorities put out advertisements for
tender for the building of the new structure and although John
Carr drew up the plans for a whole replacement structure, each
authority appointed its own contractor and the Bridge had to
be rebuilt by two different firms operating from opposite sides
of the River. Despite the rivalry between the two authorities,
the bridge was completed in the autumn of 1789 and it is a

great tribute to John Carr and the building workers that with only minor maintenance, the Green Bridge still stands today and carries a considerable amount of traffic.

The name Richmond is derived from 'riche monte' interpreted from the Norman French as a strong hill. Richmond was not mentioned in the Domesday Book by name but a recent translation of the Yorkshire section of Domesday indicates that the site was originally called 'Hindrelag'[7]. a name believed to have been changed to Richmond after the building of the Castle. However, Domesday also indicates that Hindrelag covered an area of some nine square miles containing 'a fishery and underwood', an area which would have included the sites of both Richmond and Marske.

Though conclusive evidence of the location of Hindrelag may never come to light, some guidance is available by reference to the Danish language. The Anglian Deirans who invaded and occupied Yorkshire in the 6th century, were said by Bede to have come from Jutland, or what is now the Danish peninsular. Of more particular relevance is the splitting-up of the Danish army in 874 and the action of one of their leaders named Halfdan who then moved his men to the north-east planting them in what is now Yorkshire. The numerous Danish place-names in the area, particularly those which contain personal names not otherwise found in England, give some idea of the intensity of the settlement.

It is recognised that the Danes did not intrude into the upper reaches of the Swale, yet place-names like Skeeby and Easby confirm without doubt the Danish presence in the Richmond area. In Danish, 'Hindre' means 'an obstacle' or 'obstruction', as does the German word 'Hindernis', and the Danish word 'lag' is interpreted as 'a bed of sedimentary rock.' Whilst some uncertainty may remain, there seems little doubt that the Hindrelag of Domesday was an area which included the bluff rocky site towering over the River Swale on which Earl Alan decided to build his castle.

CHAPTER VII

The Water Mills and the Trading of Woollens and Lead in Medieval Richmond

THE WATER POWER PROVIDED BY the Swale supplied no less than five Richmond corn mills, four on the River's north bank within the borough of Richmond and another on the opposite bank. All the mills ground corn and three were also used for fulling woollen cloth. Some of the mills came to be used for paper making, particularly Whitcliffe Mill, the first to be seen as the River approaches Richmond. Though the date of its origin is uncertain, a corn and fulling mill is known to have occupied this site in the 16th century and there may well have been a mill at Whitcliffe three centuries earlier. When Henry Cooke moved into the Mill in 1825 it was derelict and it took much ingenuity to re-establish it as a paper mill. He was not helped by the River Swale which flooded in 1829 and swept away much of the mill dam. The capriciousness of the River was always a disturbing element and floods in winter and droughts in summer were ever present threats.

The Swale bends as it reaches the outskirts of Richmond and here on the north bank was the Green Mill. It took its name from the The Green, the medieval suburb of Richmond. but it was also known as the Hudswell Mill after its founder William de Huddeswell. Originally built in 1354, it was rebuilt by Sir

51

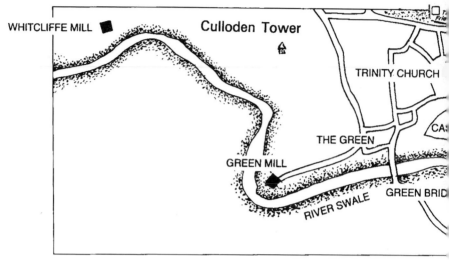

24. *The River Swale at Richmond, showing the location of the former water mills.*

William Gascoigne in 1608 and demolished in 1780. It should be mentioned that the village of Hudswell lies a short distance away on the opposite side of the River Swale. The village's history goes back to Anglian, pre-Conquest days and its name was spelt by the Normans as 'Hudreswell' — the well of Hudres, the original Anglian owner.

Dyeing and fulling were important local trades in Richmond from very early times and the Green Mill was probably founded to serve the local cloth workers. Late in the 16th and early 17th centuries Matthew Hutton, while Archbishop of York, purchased 'certain mills' in Richmond and it is known that, at the time of its demolition, the Green Mill was in the hands of the Hutton family and was being operated as a corn and fulling mill. The Green was at the centre of an industrial

52

ST MARY'S PARISH CHURCH

CHURCH MILL I

CHURCH
MILL II

ST. MARTIN'S PRIORY

CASTLE MILL

ST. MARTIN'S MILL

FALLS

area of tanners, dyers and clothmakers. A short distance down-stream from the Bridge was a dyehouse[8] which is thought to been in existence in the 12th century and to have continued operating until it was demolished in the late 18th century.

The south facing slopes below the Culloden Tower became known as the Tenter Bank for it was here that tenters were set up to serve the local clothmakers and dyers. Amongst the County clothmakers, Richmond was grouped with Bedale and Allerton and records show that Richmond was mainly concerned with the dyeing and finishing process. Cloth in the rural areas was not usually of high quality and, not having a wide appeal, it was produced mainly for local markets.

Below the south facing cliffs of Richmond Castle stood what was the most important of the water mills of Richmond, the

53

Castle Mill. It dated back to the early part of the 12th century and was sited by a natural waterfall known as the Fosse which provided power to drive the two mill wheels. Castle Mill was given to the Cistercian Abbey of Bégard in Brittany in the 12th century by one of the Earls of Richmond but objections were soon to be raised to the sending of revenues abroad. The wars with France resulted in an Act of Parliament being passed dissolving such 'alien priories' which were eventually seized by Henry IV.

In 1455/6 the Mill was rebuilt and in subsequent years it was granted to amongst others, Mount Grace Priory and Eton College. In 1606 the ownership passed for some thirty years to Timothy Hutton of Marske. He already owned the Green Mill and, by acquiring also the Castle and Church Mills he gained control of all the corn mills in Richmond except the Corporation

25. *An early picture of the Castle and Paper Mill.*
(FROM THE COLLECTION OF THE LATE LESLIE P. WENHAM)

owned Whitcliffe Mill. Timothy was succeeded by Matthew Hutton who sold both the Castle and Church Mills in 1634.

The Castle Mill[9] changed hands a number of times in subsequent years but in 1856 it was bought by James Cooke who then owned and worked the Whitcliffe Paper Mill. James was the son of Henry Cooke who had leased the Whitcliffe Mill. Some ten years after James had bought it, corn milling ceased at Castle Mill and its trade was transferred to the Church Mill, a short distance down the River. However, in 1865, James Cooke built a new paper works alongside the River front below the Castle and, prior to this — in 1821 — the Richmond Gas Light Company built one of the first gas producing installations in Europe on an adjoining site. Little now remains of these buildings except traces of the paper works as well as a brick weir half of which has been restored and, with the falls, provides an attractive tourist attraction for Richmond.

The Church Mill was probably established about 1530 on the north bank of the River but it was later rebuilt a little upstream on what is known as 'the batts'[10] and nearer to the Castle Mill site. There it survived as a corn mill until 1969, later than any other mill in Richmond.

There was another mill on the south bank of the River and that was the St Martin's Mill which belonged to St Martins Priory, a small monastic house, some ruins of which still stand between the River and the road leaving Richmond for Catterick Camp. The Priory was a cell of the great Benedictine Abbey of St Mary in York and it did not appear to have a large permanent presence of monks, the probability being that it was used primarily for elderly or convalescent brethren. St Martin's Mill continued in use long after the dissolution of the Priory and it was only finally destroyed when a railway line was constructed connecting Richmond to Darlington in 1846.

Between the 12th and 14th centuries there was a long period of prosperous trading for the high grade monastic wools produced by the Yorkshire Abbeys like Rievaulx and Fountains. Wool produced in the hill areas of the Dales was generally of lower grade but was still much in demand and quantities came into Richmond[11] for despatch to buyers either through the Tyne or Tees ports or by a recognised route from Richmond, via Bedale and Carthorpe to the Swale, Ouse and Humber.

By the 15th century, the control of wool exports came very much into the hands of the Merchants of the Staple, the most notable trade association of the time, and the law decreed that the majority of English wool had to be exported to Calais, though wool from Richmond could be sent to Holland via Newcastle. With the fall of Calais in 1558, the Merchants of the Staple turned their attention to supplying wool for the home cloth makers, the export of English cloth having developed very considerably. However, English wool was still much in demand in Europe.

When Elizabeth I came to the throne, she gave encouragement to the wearing of stockings rather than the hose previously favoured. This helped to promote a whole new hand knitting industry which developed amongst the mining communities of Swaledale as well as in the adjoining areas. For over two centuries stockings and hats, hand knitted in the Dales and around Richmond found a ready market not only in Britain but also in other countries such as Holland. Richmond, which was already a centre for wool trading, became much involved in the marketing of this local knitwear which was sent to home buyers or exported using the routes already described. For many years, the woollen industry was Richmond's largest employer.

By the beginning of the 17th century it was apparent that the export of wool had reached such proportions that supplies for home knitters in the area of Richmond and the Dales were becoming scarce and expensive. Such was the concern that a petition was sent to the House of Commons from 'the Mayor, Recorder and Aldermen of the ancient Borough of Richmond on behalf of themselves and the rest of the inhabitants of the said Borough and several poor people inhabiting in the Town adjacent'. Their complaint was that, most of the petitioners being employed in knitting woollen stockings for their support, they were no longer able to buy wool at reasonable rates because of the wool exports.

Apart from the hand knitting trade, the need to provide proper supplies of wool to the English cloth industry was now of prime importance and, in 1614, a law was passed prohibiting all further wool exports. Three years later, Richmond was named as a staple town, being one of twenty three inland towns listed in an Act of the Privy Council dated 24th March in 1617. As a result, wool began coming into Richmond[12] from a wider area than before, some from as far away as Northumberland, 'to be viewed, weighed and registered for the preventing of all fraudes and abuses which are daily practised both in the commodity itself and in the indirect disposing thereof'. Apart from applying a check on the wool being produced, the purpose was to prevent it from being exported and to direct the wool to the home cloth making industries.

The staple towns nominated were regarded as being convenient to the 'cloth country' as well as being remote from the sea and the exporting ports. However, the movement of wool to Richmond and other appointed staple towns over long distances created some problems. In 1701 a further petition was made to the House of Commons by the inhabitants of Richmond and other adjacent parts complaining that, under existing law, no wool was to be carried 'between Sun and Sun' meaning only in daylight hours. The penalty for breaking this law was the forfeiture of both the wool and the carrier's horse.

The petition pointed out that carriers bringing wool from as far away as Northumberland were often within sight of their destination when the sun went down yet they could not complete the last stage of their journey for fear of having their wool seized. The Commons agreed to inspect the law but they were clearly worried that wool might be taken to ports for illegal export under cover of darkness.

Apart from the wool and knitwear trading, Richmond was much involved in marketing lead from the Swaledale and Arkengarthdale area. There was demand from the monastic houses for lead for building purposes and as early as 1300, pack-horse loads of lead were being brought down to Richmond for sale in the open market. There is reference in the books of York Guildhall describing a shipment of Swaledale lead being brought through Richmond and by road and river to York in 1560-1. During the peak periods of lead mining in the 18th and 19th centuries a great deal of lead passed through Richmond for export using the Tees at Worsall, Yarm and Stockton, the ports of Newcastle and Hull and the rivers Swale and Ure to reach the Humber.

After the railway was built to Richmond, lead was carried by horses to Richmond station. From there, it was moved to Darlington before being routed to Yarm, Stockton or on to Newcastle. Lead at that time was usually stamped with the initials and mark of the mining company concerned as for instance the A.D. Company which took over the Gunnerside Gill St Francis mine and sent quantities of lead stamped with their mark to countries like Sweden, Holland and Germany.

The mining[13] of copper clearly played an important part in Richmond's history as far back as the late 15th century. In 1578 a Mr Humphrey Cole[14] of London presented the Lord Treasurer with 'a piece of green ore' which had been found in a quarry in the grounds of Mr Robert Bowes at Aske near Richmond and made it known that there were rich deposits of copper to be had 'in the hills thereabouts'. Robert Bowes is recorded as having been Queen Elizabeth's treasurer and ambassador to Scotland. At a later time, copper was indeed mined on the boundary between Richmond Racecourse and Gingerfield Farm, adjacent to Aske Estate. A William Chayter who took out a lease on this mine in 1758 became involved in a dispute of ownership with Lord Dundas of Aske Hall but this was eventually settled by an agreement to divide the copper extracted from the mine.

By this time, copper mining had also developed a few miles away at Middleton Tyas and on the north side of the River Swale in the area of Whitcliffe Woods. However, the earliest mining took place at Billy Bank wood on the south bank of the River nearly opposite the site of the old Green Mill. Here a copper vein had been exposed by the scour of the River and mining is known to have started towards the end of the 15th century. It continued with some periods of inactivity until the mine finally closed in 1912. It is estimated that there were some 4,000 feet of passages in the mine. Despite the proximity to the River there seems to have been little difficulty with flooding though water in the rock strata created considerable problems for the miners.

The guilds of Richmond in the medieval period were of very considerable importance and they controlled much of the trade and government of the town. Members of the Guild of Fellmongers were particularly important as they were involved not only in buying and selling sheepskins but also general wool trading.[15] It is interesting that, following the discovery in 1981 of its early records, the Fellmongers Company of Richmond has now been reconstituted. This and the Guild of Mercers, Grocers and Haberdashers are still in existence in Richmond today.

CHAPTER VIII

Scots Dyke, Easby, Colburn, the Medieval Hospital of St Giles and Brough Hall

As THE SWALE REACHES THE eastern boundaries of Richmond, it passes perhaps the best preserved section of the extraordinary Scots Dyke earthwork. Linear bank-and-ditch earthworks of the Anglo-Saxon age have been found in many parts of the country some being constructed primarily as boundaries and others being clearly intended for defensive purposes. In Cambridgeshire, for instance, a system of dykes crossed the open chalk country between fen and wood and was probably built for defensive purposes by the Anglians against the Mercians. The Scots Dyke earthwork may have been built by the Britons in the 5th century as a boundary. Recent aerial photography indicates that the Dyke was probably part of a network continuing northwards through Durham and Northumberland, possibly connecting with the Catrail in southern Scotland.

The view that Scots Dyke assumed a defensive role could be supported by the apparent existence of a ditch on the east side of the earthwork. As mentioned in Chapter 4 it is possible that, after crossing the Swale near St Martin's, the Dyke veered westwards and after reaching Fremington, crossed the River at Grinton. An interesting find near the Dyke has been an

Anglian spear-head which is now in the Richmondshire Museum.

It is generally accepted that Swaledale ends at Richmond after which the River begins its journey through the more lowland countryside leading into the Vale of York. However, the stretch of the River between Richmond and Easby has a particular beauty. Here the banks are well wooded and, moving in a southerly direction, the Swale reaches the peaceful setting of Easby Abbey. Here also is the old Church of St Agatha of Sicily who was martyred at Catania in A.D. 251. The Church is mainly 13th century with later additions but it is known that a building existed on the site probably in Anglian times and certainly before the Abbey was created.

St Agatha's Church is a place of remarkable peace and beauty. By the entrance is a carved Norman font and on the

26. Easby Abbey – the remains of the Refectory in which was the reader's pulpit.

walls of the chancel are historic frescoes depicting Adam and Eve in the Garden of Eden, their fall and driving out to till the ground. On the opposite wall, the frescoes depict the adoration of the shepherds and the Magi, the descent from the Cross, the burial and resurrection. There is also the plaster cast of what has come to be known as the Easby Cross, the original of which dates back to the late 7th or early 8th century and which is now to be found in London at the Victoria and Albert Museum.

There is an interesting link between St Agatha's and the Swale family of Grinton for an epitaph was found in the Church giving thanks for the life of one Richard Swale.[16] The epitaph which was clearly in favour of the Reformation was written in Hebrew, Greek, Latin and English in the period before the reign of Henry VIII. This was a time when it was dangerous to propagate religious opinions hostile to the Church of Rome.

The Premonstratensian Abbey of Easby was founded about 1155 by Roald who was the Constable of Richmond Castle. The Premonstratensian Order started in France in 1120 and, though members of the Order were required to live a life of poverty and chastity, they were not monks living a life shut off from the outside world. Indeed. they were allowed to leave the cloister of the Abbey and go out to preach and minister to the people of the world outside. Because of their white clothing they were known as the white canons.

Easby was the earliest Premonstratensian Abbey to be founded in this area of Yorkshire. There were others at Coverham and Egglestone.Though Easby's sheep farming and wool production did in no way reach the levels of the big Cistercian abbeys like Fountains and Rievaulx, wool sales would have provided a useful income. The Abbey had considerable grazing land in the area and at one time it is recorded as having had no less than nine granges which were used for arable or sheep farming and yielded a sizeable rent for the Abbey. In common with other northern monasteries its property and revenue suffered from the plundering raids of the Scots and, in 1346, the English army on its way to the Battle of Neville's Cross caused great damage to Easby as well as to its sister monastery at Egglestone.

Whilst Easby was recompensed to some extent for this damage, it was also helped in 1393 by the acquisition of the patronage by Sir Henry Scrope whose son later increased its endowment to give support to ten more canons as well as founding a chantry in the monastic church. The generous gifts made by local benefactors are indeed reflected in the size and extent of the buildings of this historic Abbey which continued to minister to the people until 1537 when Henry VIII ordered its closure. Those who visit the ruins of the monastery today cannot fail to appreciate the skill and ingenuity of the medieval builders who created such a place.

The location[17] of the Abbey by the Swale at Easby has been referred to by the late Richmond historian Leslie P. Wenham in a rather different context. In the mid 19th century, Mr Ralph M. Jacques of Easby Hall maintained an extensive and successful racing stud by the side of the Swale using 'a most secluded part of the ruins'. His successes included four Derby winners and one of his much prized horses named Emilius lies buried near the Abbey — 'in a small paddock by the river side, formed out of the Abbey ruins; and there is an old crosiered tombstone placed in the wall to denote the resting place of one of the most celebrated horses of the British turf'.

From Easby, the River passes under a bridge which carried the now dismantled railway, turns to the east and is soon joined by Colburn Beck. The village of Colburn stands high to the south of the Swale and its most notable building is Colburn Hall. Though now a farmstead, this historic Hall, thought to have originally been of 14th century structure, was the seat of the D'Arcys. They were an ancient Catholic family and in 1537 Thomas Lord D'Arcy suffered death for his participation in the

Pilgrimage of Grace. He was one of many devoted catholics who took part in the rebellion and met their end. Another was Sir Francis Bigod a Swaledale landowner of Healaugh who was beheaded and there was also Anthony Peacock,[18] a local rebel of Arkengarthdale, who was hanged on Richmond Moor for his activities. They were victims of the process of retribution demanded by Henry VIII and enforced with severity by Thomas Cromwell and the Duke of Norfolk.

Close to Colburn Hall, there is another interesting building dated about 1300 which is thought to have been used as a courthouse from which the medieval manor was administered. The main room of this ancient building is on the first floor which is reached by external steps and there has been a particularly fine window in the south wall.

On the south side of the Swale as it approaches Brompton, the remains have been found of the medieval hospital of St Giles. The existence of this hospital dates back as far as 1181 and it may have been established a little earlier. It was sited by an important medieval crossing of the River on what was the road linking Swaledale with the Vale of York. Recent excavation and research by Mr Peter Cardwell and others on behalf of North Yorkshire County Council has revealed that, though this was only a relatively small medieval hospital, it played an important part in the early history of this area until about 1500. Its importance may have begun to decline however when a new bridge was constructed in 1421/2 crossing the River Swale at Catterick Bridge.

St Giles hospital may originally have consisted of no more than a chapel and a hall but it developed into a complex of five or six buildings. Whereas the chapel was stone built, the hall and subsequent buildings were probably of timber construction on a stone foundation. The original chapel was replaced about 1300 by a larger building and a tower or belfry was erected later. Though the importance of St Giles had waned by

27. *The excavated remains of St Giles Hospital chapel.*
(BY PERMISSION OF PETER CARDWELL)

the year 1500, it seems likely that the chapel had some continued use, the Catterick area being known as a centre for Catholicism.

Unlike modern hospitals concerned only with treating the sick, medieval hospitals like St Giles would have served a variety of functions. They were primarily religious houses giving care to the soul as well as the body and they are known to have provided a home for the elderly, medical care for the sick, alms for the poor and, certainly at St Giles, hospitality for the traveller. In medieval England there were over 700 hospitals and though most were near towns, those in rural areas like St Giles were usually situated close to main highways.

It is evident that the hospital was administered by a master who would have been a priest and the names of two masters are known, John de Ellerton in 1306 and Walter de Wensley in

1376. The master would probably have had the assistance of another priest and of some lay brothers and sisters and the hospital would have been run on monastic lines. Strangely, though St Giles was one of the most popular saints in Western Europe in the Middle Ages, little is known about him, except that he lived as a hermit in southern France about A.D. 800 and that he became the patron saint of cripples and the infirm.

It is interesting that the investigations into this St Giles site not only revealed the existence of a medieval hospital but also evidence of some bronze or early iron age occupation of the River terrace. In 1574, the site passed into the hands of the Lawson family as part of the manor of Brough and in 1650, the remains of the hospital building were converted into a farm-stead.

According to Clarkson, Catterick Bridge was rebuilt in 1421 'at the expense of 260 marks and a few gowns to the workmen', replacing an earlier wooden bridge. At the south end of the bridge was placed a small chapel dedicated to St Ann.[19] Here, Mass was said every day by a priest from the Hospital of St Giles at 12 o'clock 'for the use of travellers praying for a pros-perous journey and where alms were received by way of con-tribution towards the repair of the bridge'.It seems likely that this chapel of St Ann, as well as the St Giles chapel, continued in use for some time after the demise of the hospital. The Chapel of St Ann was eventually demolished at a time when the stone bridge was widened and then rebuilt. The bridge now crosses the Swale by the present Catterick Bridge Hotel, on the site of which was an old coaching house known as the George Inn.

Beyond the site of the Hospital of St Giles and standing high on the fertile plain south of the River is Brough Hall. This 15th century building is believed to have originated as a medieval fortified tower. The Hall was the home of the de Burgh family who are believed to have taken their name from the town of Brough. Records show that Richard de Richmond who

28. *The Chapel of St Ann, Catterick Bridge.*
(FROM THE COLLECTION OF THE LATE LESLIE P. WENHAM)

67

married a Burgh heiress in the 14th century was the principal architect of his family's rise into the country gentry. It is known that he took the name de Burgh and, being Catholics, the family kept a low profile at the time of the Pilgrimage of Grace. In 1574 Sir Ralph Lawson married Elizabeth de Burgh and the estate passed to the Lawsons.

Sir Ralph and his wife did much to turn Brough Hall into an Elizabethan mansion but it was in the more peaceful 18th century that the great house and park underwent the most extensive alteration. In the 1730s, the first baronet's grandson, another Sir John, is thought to have given the house a classical appearance. He also built a chapel in a new wing and further additions were made by a later generation of the Lawsons. The family continued to be pillars of the Roman Catholic community and, within a few weeks of inheriting Brough Hall in 1834 and following the passing of the Catholic Emancipation Act, William Lawson built a new Roman Catholic church on the Brough Hall Park estate. It was designed in consultation

29. *The church dedicated to St Paulinus at Brough Hall.*

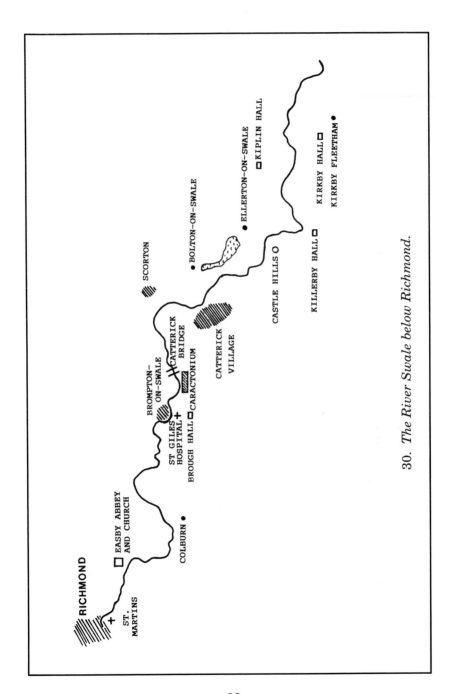

30. *The River Swale below Richmond.*

with the Durham architect Ignatius Bonomi and was modelled on the 13th century chapel of the Archbishop of York. The Church was dedicated to St Paulinus, the saint who baptised thousands of people in the River Swale nearby.

Reaching Brompton, the River describes a half circle round the village. Brompton on Swale is known to be sited on what was once an Anglian settlement under the dominance of the important base at Gilling. However, the discovery in 1963 of an iron age sword during quarrying operations nearby suggests that the site may have been occupied in even earlier times. The sword was of the Halstatt type dated between 550 and 500 B.C.

A 12th century bridge over the River at Brompton is mentioned in the records though this could have been the crossing leading to St Giles Hospital or, as Clarkson suggests, the nearby Catterick bridge. Brompton also had an ancient water mill which was noted in the Domesday Book and a drawing of the mill is preserved at the York Minster Library.

CHAPTER IX

Historic Catterick

IT IS AFTER LEAVING BROMPTON on Swale that the River reaches Catterick and an area of extraordinary historical interest. The Brigantes were probably the first to come here and they called it 'Cat-Rhych' or a camp on a ridge. They are known to have made their settlements close by river crossings. Catterick Bridge as we know it today adjoins the site of what was an important Roman fort and town known as Cataractonium.

It was in the first century A.D. and probably during the governorship of Agricola that the Romans came to Catterick. Sited by Dere Street, the main Roman road linking York with Hadrians Wall and with a branch route over the Pennines, the commanders must have realised that it had considerable strategic importance and could control egress from Swaledale. There is no doubt that Catterick continued to be a focal point of importance long after the Romans had departed.

The Romans chose what has become known as the Thornborough plateau site standing high above the south bank of the Swale, near the point where Dere Street crossed the River and to the west of Catterick Bridge. There they built an Agricolan fort. This was evacuated for a period about A.D. 120, and a complex[20] building thought to be a mansio, or inn, was then constructed on the site of the fort bath-house. The mansio seems to have been built to a very high standard and contained

71

a series of rooms arranged in two main suites each with its own principal room and piped water supply.

By A.D. 160 however the fort had been re-occupied, the mansio was dismantled and a civilian settlement began to develop with timber framed buildings which were later rebuilt in stone. Between the 3rd and 4th centuries, a substantial defensive stone wall was built, together with an outer ditch, which encircled both the fort and the civilian area.

Though discoveries of several Romano-British artefacts had been made in earlier times, the first recorded excavation on the Thornborough site was undertaken in the early part of the 19th century when Sir William Lawson of Brough Hall excavated along the lines of the east, south and west sections of the wall. In 1625, a large bronze cauldron full of Roman coins was found. Other finds have included a buckle plate, three Anglo-Saxon brooches of the 6th century, and two stone lions found on the line of the Roman road.

More recently, much of the available information about Cataractonium has come from a series of excavations undertaken by John Wacher following earlier work by E.J.W. Hildyard. This excavation work had been prompted by the A1 motorway developments and with the use of aerial photography invaluable evidence was provided giving the location of early buildings. Though most of these buildings were later submerged under the Catterick by-pass, the considerable research work carried out in past years has enabled us to formulate an accurate picture of this important Roman centre.

Research has shown that, by the early part of the 4th century, the few houses surrounding the fort at Cataractonium had been replaced by a small town with houses and shops. Many of the buildings excavated were shown to have been built early in the 4th century but, about A.D. 370, a further major rebuilding took place which radically changed the whole nature of the

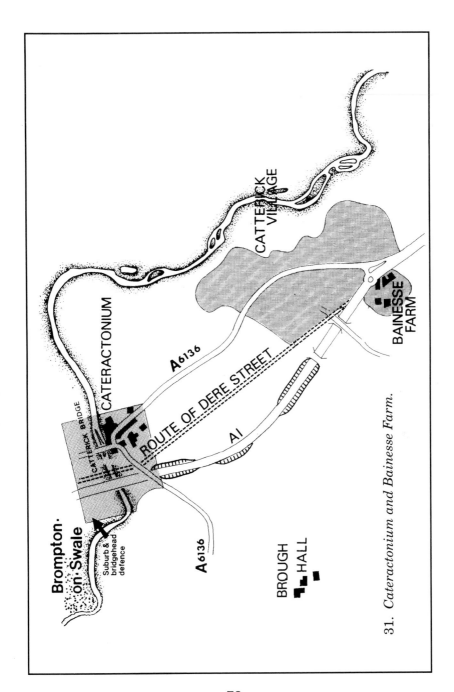

31. *Cateractonium and Bainesse Farm.*

town. A new road was made and almost all the shops were re-built on different alignments and without open fronts. New shops were added and a group of buildings formed a unified complex grouped round an 'L' shaped courtyard. Entrance to this courtyard from the north was by a great gate spanning about 9 ft. As J.S. Wacher has pointed out, this small town was amongst the last examples of Roman coordinated town planning.

A military tannery, probably associated with the fort, was found on a downhill slope to the east and a small bath-house[21] was located which did not seem to have been used and may not have been fully completed. This bath-house with its surrounding buildings was probably erected in the first half of the third century and it was in a remarkable state of preservation. The surrounding buildings appeared to have been used for domestic purposes.

The present village of Catterick stands about one mile to the south of Cataractonium and on the site of what the Romans referred to as Caer Cateraie, interpreted as the Catterick of the Britons. The village has its 15th century perpendicular Church of St Anne which was built in 1412 with funds provided by the De Burgh family. In the north aisle of the church there are some interesting memorial brasses of the De Burghs. It is thought that an earlier Anglian church in the village was burnt down and replaced by a stone building, much of the stone being used later to build the walls of the present church.

Excavation has been carried out nearby on what is known as the Bainesse Farm site, mainly to the east of the Roman Dere Street. This proved to be a roadside settlement with an accompanying field system occupied by the Romans between the 1st and 3rd centuries. The reason for the existence of this settlement so near to Cataractonium is unclear. However, it evidently flourished, presumably by farming the field system and by being near the Roman Dere Street. The site seems to have been abandoned towards the end of the 3rd century and this may have coincided with the building of a defensive wall encircling Cataractonium. Perhaps the circumstances of that time encouraged the Bainesse peoples to seek the security of the nearby town. Whilst the settlement still presents some unsolved problems for the historians, there is also difficulty in explaining the existence of a sizeable Anglo-Saxon burial ground discovered a short distance to the north-west of Bainesse.

At Pallett Hill which adjoins Catterick village, evidence has been found of an iron age settlement and no doubt a base there was well positioned between the iron age strongholds of Stanwick and York. Here there also appears to have been a motte[22] and bailey castle.

Whereas the excavation of the fort and town of Cataractonium south of the River Swale has attracted much attention over the years, the same can be said of the town's northern suburb across the River. The early occupation by the Brigantes has already been mentioned and work by a Richmondshire Excavation Group not only revealed evidence of a 3rd century road and civil occupation, but also the existence of an apparent flood defence system.

Subsequent investigation brought to light a gravel and cobbled causeway leading to the River. It is thought unlikely that this causeway provided a route to a ford across the Swale and no trace has been found of a bridge being built at this point. More likely is the opinion that the causeway served some form of wharfage along the north bank of the River. This is supported by the knowledge that, as described earlier, wool and lead were known to be transported by river in the 13th and 14th century period using the Swale at or above Myton.It is a reasonable assumption that, some 1200 years earlier, the Swale was navigable up river as far as Catterick using shallow draught vessels.

There is no doubt that, if indeed the Swale were navigable up to Catterick, it would have been of considerable importance to the area. The availability of cheap water transport would have allowed the export of the bulk products of the region and would have provided a point of access for goods from other parts of Britain and abroad. Cataractonium could well have performed the function of an entrepôt for a considerable area.

The Romans came to Britain in A.D. 43 and they remained for a period of nearly four hundred years. It was one of the most important periods in our history, and their considerable bequest to us includes a system of administration which was clearly effective in Cataractonium and is still recognised in our way of life today.

Postscript October 1995:

In 1995, excavations near Catterick racecourse have revealed the remains of a Roman amphitheatre. This is a remarkable find as the only other known amphitheatres were built in major Roman centres like Chester. The find serves to emphasise the importance of Cataractonium.

CHAPTER X

The Arrival of the Anglians

EVEN BEFORE THE ROMAN DEPARTURE, there had been plundering raids from across the North Sea and, without the Roman
defence system, it was soon apparent that the Romano-British
who remained were incapable of withstanding further invasions from mainland Europe. A new era in the history of Britain
was about to begin. Described by some historians as a forma-
tive period, it was a time of invasion and gradual settlement
by various groups from the Germanic and Scandinavian countries.

Unlike the more secluded country of the Dale above
Richmond, the Lower Swale flows through an area which for
centuries lay in the path of successive invading forces.
Consequently, though the River area here has many places of
interest to describe, its history must take into account the
records of the Germanic invasions, the Scandinavians and the
Normans.

Firstly, there came the Anglo-Saxons, and then, several centuries later, the Danes and the Norsemen. Though it was a long
chapter of invasion, plunder, destruction and ruthless battles
between contending kings, it was also a time for the development of Christianity. The area served by the Lower Swale
played no small part in making the history of those violent
times and the strategic importance of Catterick proved to be
as important to the Anglo-Saxons as it had been to the Romans.

The 5th century invaders of Britain are frequently described as Anglo-Saxons though they were in fact Saxons, Anglians, Jutes and perhaps some Frisians. They all belonged to a single group of related Germanic nations yet those who first came to Britain are known to have claimed individual identity regarding themselves as, for instance, Anglians or Saxons. In recounting the chain of events which led to the Germanic occupation of the River Swale area it should be recalled that the first invaders of North Eastern Britain were Anglians though, as time progressed, the influence of the Saxons became more evident particularly with the spread of Christianity. The whole of the River Swale and its hinterland became a part of the Anglian kingdom of Deira which later linked with its northerly neighbour Bernicia, to form the larger kingdom of Northumbria.

Our knowledge of Anglo-Saxon history and certainly of the Anglian and subsequent intrusions has been very dependent on the writings of the Venerable Bede and to a lesser extent those of Symeon of Durham as well as Gildas, a 6th century monk. These sources have described to us the events leading to and following the Anglian occupation and the influence of Paulinus in developing Christianity in the area of the River Swale and elsewhere.

In about A.D. 449, a certain British Chieftain named Vortigern enlisted the help of two Saxons to cross the sea and help repel the raids of the Picts and Scots. The brothers Hengest and Horsa came with their mercenaries but were soon to turn against their employers after a disagreement about their rations. Soon more Germanic intruders landed in Britain and there began a period of ruthless slaughter and plunder throughout the countryside. Ultimately, a large part of Eastern England was taken over and held by the invaders.

Before the end of the 5th century, Anglians who had invaded the country south of the River Humber began to move north and established themselves in what we know as Central and Eastern Yorkshire. They were the Deirans who, according to Bede, came to Britain from a country called Angulus, or Jutland, with its neighbouring islands.

These Deirans settled initially on the Yorkshire Wolds near Beverley. Any plans they may have had for expansion to the west were thwarted for some time by the Britons of Elmet but archaeological evidence suggests that they reached York by the year 500 A.D. The rate of their progress northwards is uncertain, but they reached Ripon and, using the Roman roadways, they moved northwards to Catterick and beyond. Though they are known to have inhabited parts of Wensleydale, there are no records of the Anglians moving into Swaledale towards Reeth until the late 7th century and the people of the Dales seemed to go largely unmolested for a considerable period.

North of the River Tyne, Anglians known as the Bernicians had become established on the coast using Bamburgh as their stronghold. For many years they lived precariously on their coastal strip but eventually they began to move inland and became a formidable enemy to the older celtic kingdoms of the Forth and Clyde valleys. By the year 600 they were still fighting with the celtic Scots but they gradually spread over the whole area to the Solway in the west and down to the River Tees in the east.

The conflict between the British and the invading Anglians reached a peak in 570 when Catterick was the site of a bitter battle which did much to decide who was in control in northern Britain. The story of this encounter is told in a famous Welsh poem 'Gododdin' which related that a force of young British warriors was sent down by the celtic ruler of the country round Edinburgh to attack the Anglian invaders. Additional support was provided by celtic men from the Solway and Morecambe Bay who joined the force from Edinburgh to fight the Deirans. The Welsh poem recites that, when the two sides

79

clashed at Cattraeth, generally accepted as being Catterick, they fought a bloodthirsty battle which lasted for a week. In the end, the Britons were routed and only a few of their number survived the encounter.

The original Kingdom of Deira is known to have covered the area between the Humber and the Tees.It was not until the beginning of the 7th century that Deira and Bernicia were joined to form Northumbria under a Bernician King named Aethelfrith. Though the Bernicians had in fact brought these two Germanic Anglian peoples together, for which Bede gave praise to King Aethelfrith, there was always an undercurrent of strife between them. This had its origins in a feud which existed about the way each was descended from the god Woden.Though the two were clearly of equal ancestry much of their early history turns on their continued rivalry.

An important stage in history occurred when King Aethelfrith was killed in battle and Edwin, the heir to the Deiran throne, was declared King of Northumbria. For some years Edwin had lived in exile in various places including, in Aethelfrith's reign, a period as a guest of Raedwald, king of the East Angles. This did not please Aethelfrith who demanded that Edwin should be killed or surrendered. Raewald's wife however persuaded her husband that a man of honour could not betray his guest and, in the end, it was resolved to find a way to take Edwin back to his own kingdom. This failure to agree to Aethelfrith's demands was to lead to inevitable conflict and it proved to be the first recorded trial of strength between a king of Northumbria and a ruler who had become supreme in England south of the Humber. A battle took place on the southern borders of Deira and Aethelfrith who had been unable to bring all his men together for the conflict was killed, his sons having to flee into exile.

This victory resulted in Edwin being accepted as king of both Deira and Bernicia and, within a few years, he became

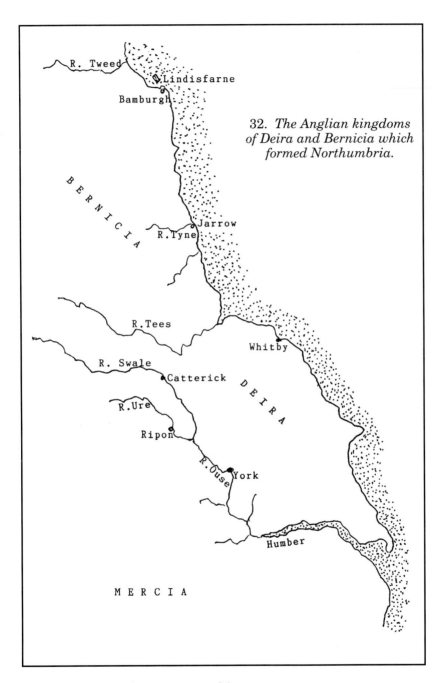

R. Tweed

Lindisfarne

Bamburgh

32. *The Anglian kingdoms of Deira and Bernicia which formed Northumbria.*

B E R N I C I A

Jarrow

R. Tyne

R. Tees

Whitby

R. Swale

Catterick

D E I R A

R. Ure

Ripon

R. Ouse

York

Humber

M E R C I A

the successor to Raedwald as overlord of all English people south of the Humber. Edwin has been described as a typical king of the Heroic Age. He liked to follow Roman ceremonial custom and it is believed that a standard bearer rode before him on his journeys to places like Catterick and he was preceded by a banner of the type the Romans called a 'tufa'.

As related in the following chapter this pagan King Edwin was to marry the Christian Princess Aethelberga of Kent and, after a period, he also accepted the Christian faith. Their marriage led to the arrival of Paulinus and the subsequent conversion to Christianity of a great many people of the River Swale.

CHAPTER XI

Paulinus and the Holy River Swale

THE STORY OF PAULINUS COULD be said to start in the year 596
A.D. when Pope Gregory sent St Augustine to England to
preach Christianity to the people. Augustine first preached in
the Isle of Thanet to the Saxon King Aethelberht of Kent who
accepted the Christian doctrine and was baptised. Augustine
continued to preach to the people of Kent but he soon needed
more assistance in his task, and two of his followers named
Lawrence and Peter were despatched to Rome with a plea to
Pope Gregory to provide 'fresh labourers for the vineyard'. After
a year's delay at Rome, the Pope sent back two messengers
accompanied by twelve new apostles to work in developing the
Church in Anglo-Saxon Britain. The party is said to have
reached Marseilles from Rome and then journeyed on through
the diocese of Toulouse to Metz and Paris, finally reaching Kent
where the travellers were honourably received by King
Aethelberht. Included in the party was a monk named Paulinus
of whom little was then heard for the next twenty four years.
Yet his name was then to become closely linked with
Northumbria and the country of the River Swale.

In 625 A.D. the ambassadors of the pagan King Edwin of
Northumbria arrived in Kent to acquire the hand of King
Aethelberht's daughter Aethelberga. The King's reply was that
it was not lawful to give a Christian virgin in marriage to a

heathen. Edwin, said by Bede to be a 'man of no common temper', took no offence at the answer and sent his ambassadors a second time with the promise that he would take no steps against the Christian faith and would grant the princess and her retinue free exercise of their religion. Should the new faith be found to be more worthy he would himself embrace it. This was accepted by King Aethelberht and the marriage with his daughter, affectionately known as Tata, was duly arranged.

The Pope had ordered that two Synods be established, one in London and the other in York each with twelve suffragan bishops. However, London was later replaced by Canterbury with papal agreement. It was Paulinus who was chosen to go to York, a see which was to enjoy metropolitan status. He was consecrated[23] Bishop of York and, having accepted the role of Aethelberga's spiritual father, he accompanied her on the journey north to York.

Once established in York it became clear that Paulinus was not going to confine himself to supporting Aethelberga and her attendants and he began to work unceasingly to spread the gospel of Christianity amongst the people. His labours at first met with little success and many months were to pass before Edwin was persuaded to become a Christian and be baptised, though Paulinus had reminded him of his promise prior to the marriage.

On the eve of Easter in the year 626 A.D. Edwin miraculously escaped an attempt at assassination which was thwarted by his servant Lilla, and Aethelberga bore him a daughter whom they called Eanflaed. It was then Edwin vowed that, should he be successful in war, he would agree to become a Christian. In the meantime, he allowed his infant daughter Eanflaed as well as eleven members of his family to be baptised on Whitsuntide of that year. Raising his army the King then marched against the West Saxons who had conspired to

33. *Bishop Paulinus as depicted in a window of York Minster.*
(REPRODUCED WITH PERMISSION OF YORK MINSTER LIBRARY)

murder him. Returning victorious, he received a letter from the Pope urging him to accept the Christian faith.

Summoning a council of his 'friends, princes and counsellors' he sought their agreement to accept Christianity so that they might all be baptised together. There was some debate but with the support of the chief of the King's priests, agreement was reached. On Easter Eve in the following year Edwin was baptised by Paulinus in York at the wooden church of St Peter the Apostle which Edwin had built for the occasion. On the same day, Paulinus baptised Hilda under whose guidance the monastery at Whitby became a most important and influential centre of Christianity.

As soon as he was baptised and with guidance from Bishop Paulinus, Edwin set about building a larger and nobler stone church which legend tells us was on the site of what is now York Minster. From a Christian point of view, the following six years were of considerable importance to Northumbria and East Anglia. Often accompanied by Paulinus, the King made frequent visits to his dominions. which included Bernicia, Deira and East Anglia. Paulinus continued to preach and convert the people though he had some difficulty in evangelising the Bernicians. There were no churches outside York and he baptised his converts in rivers like the Glen near Wooler and the River Trent in Nottinghamshire. In Yorkshire however,he spent much time in the area of the Swale and it was there that he reaped his greatest harvest.

By the 7th century, Catterick had gained a new importance as one of the royal vills of Northumbria and, according to Bede, it was 'in the rocky pools of the ancient cataract' of the Swale at Catterick that Paulinus baptised great multitudes of the people. The flow of the River has changed over the centuries but it is evident that, having blessed the waters, Paulinus baptised his many converts, probably in the stretch of the Swale above Catterick Bridge. He also preached and converted the people further down the Swale at Brafferton. Here, wrote Camden, Paulinus blessed the River and directed the converts to go in two by two and baptise each other in the name of the Holy Trinity. It was no small wonder that the Swale came to be regarded as a Holy River and that to some it was the Jordan of England.

By 627 A.D. Paulinus had come to possess a church in Lincoln and it was there that he consecrated Honorius as the new Archbishop of Canterbury. As he was probably the only bishop in England at that time Paulinus was the proper person to consecrate the elect of Canterbury. Moreover, his success in establishing Christianity in Edwin's kingdom was soon to be recognised by the Pope with the establishment of an archbishopric of York and Paulinus became the first Archbishop of this northern province.

While Paulinus laboured to bring a rapid extension of Christianity to the area, King Edwin had ruled peacefully and well for some seventeen years bringing Northumbria to the height of its power. However, it was an era which came to an end when Cadwallon of Wessex with support from Penda King of Mercia, decided to attack Edwin and his Kingdom. A battle was fought at Hatfield near Doncaster and Edwin was killed. As one of his sons was also slain and another killed later, it was the end of Edwin's branch of the royal house of Deira.

There followed a period of savage cruelty when Cadwallon and Penda set out to devastate Northumbria. It was a disaster for the church and brought persecution for Northumbrian Christians. Edwin's kingdom immediately fell apart into its two fundamental divisions of Deira and Bernicia. Paulinus might have remained with his church but he reverted to his office of guardian of Aethelburga. With no prospect of safety except in flight, he decided to take ship with Aethelburga and her children and with an escort of Bassus,one of Edwins closest warriors, they sailed for Kent. At that time, a voyage by sea was always slow and dangerous yet it was probably quicker and indeed safer than a long journey overland across several kingdoms which could well be at war with each other. It is interesting that, some years later, one of Edwin's children Eanflaed made a return journey by sea to become a queen in her turn.

Paulinus took with him a large gold cross and golden chalice for preservation in Canterbury and, on their arrival in Kent, he and Queen Aethelberga were well received by King Eadbald. At that time, the Bishop of Rochester had been sent on a mission to the Pope but was drowned at sea. The bishopric having become vacant in this way, Paulinus was appointed and held the position until his death in the year 644.

As a man, he was remembered as a tall figure, slightly bent, with a hooked nose and an emaciated face. His work in Northumbria being cut short as it was, it seems probable that Christianity was not sufficiently well established to withstand Cadwallon's persecution. Yet the seeds had been sown and Paulinus left James the deacon behind him in his Church in York. James bravely remained at his post during that difficult period. In 633 A.D. Cadwallon was slain by the christian King Oswald and, as more peaceful times returned, James converted and baptised the Deirons, teaching them to chant in the Roman manner. He is said by Bede to have continued to live in a village by the Swale near Catterick until the end of his days.

CHAPTER XII

The Warrior Kings and the Arrival of the Scandinavians

"....War's a game which, were their subjects wise,
Kings would not play at..."

(William Cowper 1731-1800)

AFTER THE DEATH OF CADWALLON in 633, both Deira and Bernicia were ruled by King Oswald. He was descended from the older Deiran Kings and he held the position of Head of the Bernician Royal House. He proved to be a great Christian King and the people living by the River Swale would have benefited by the stability which he brought. However, his reign proved to be all too short for, after only eight years, he was defeated and killed in a battle with Penda of Mercia. Oswald was held in such respect that he was immediately recognised as a saint and martyr.

The following years of the 7th century saw many periods of violence and change. The kings of that time, described as warrior kings, were warlords in an age when men lived by the sword and saw it as their duty to enlarge and defend their kingdoms by winning battles. Some kings were more warlike than others but most reigned only for a limited number of years before meeting their deaths. Though those who followed in the

8th and into the 9th centuries were less concerned with enlarging their kingdoms, they were much more involved in internal strife and dynastic feuds.

Although Penda gained power by his defeat of Oswald, Deira and Bernicia separated and proceeded to choose their own kings. Bernicia's choice of Oswald's brother as their King roused the ire of Penda who led a large force to attack the Bernicians. In the battle which followed, Penda was killed and his forces were defeated. The age of the warrior kings continued and, although much of the violence appears to have occurred in Bernicia, Deira with the River Swale was not immune from change. The King they originally chose, named Oswine, was soon out of favour and he was removed. There were raids into the Northumbrian area from Mercia, expeditions against the Picts and a series of internal revolutions which when resolved, left Northumbria as a single state again with its northern boundary reaching to the Firth of Forth.

The work of Paulinus in teaching the Christian faith was rebuffed by Cadwallon but encouraged during King Oswald's short reign. For a period, the restoration of Christianity became vested in the Celtic rather than the Roman Church, firstly by St Aidan and then by St Cuthbert who became Bishop of Lindisfarne and whose remains were eventually laid to rest in Durham Cathedral. Though the Bishopric of York, but not the Archbishopric, was restored in 663 it was not until 735 that a second Archbishop was consecrated. Despite the era of warrior kings and the political confusion which resulted, it is apparent that there was remarkable little interference with monastic learning in Northumbria during these unsettled times.

It was in the year 787 that the Anglo-Saxon Chronicle recorded the landing of the first Scandinavian invaders who came from Norway and raided the coast of Dorset. There followed the plundering of Lindisfarne in A.D. 793 and Jarrow in the following year. Yet the main body of the Norwegian adventurers passed round the North of Scotland, some settling in Shetland, Orkney, the Faroe Islands and Iceland. Many came down the west coast of Scotland however and settled in Ireland and the Isle of Man. It was not until the 10th century that these Norsemen began crossing the sea to reach North West England some then finding their way over the Pennines to settle in Upper Swaledale.

Though there had been a number of plunderous raids beforehand, it was not until A.D. 865 that a considerable Danish army landed in East Anglia where they remained for twelve months obtaining horses and generally consolidating their position. Their method of operation was to seize a defensive position, fortify it and then ravage the surrounding countryside systematically. They did this in East Anglia and they then moved up to York which they occupied in the autumn of 866 evidently taking pleasure in destroying religious houses and using the old Roman fortifications for their protection. They then moved further north through the area of the River Swale and beyond. These Danes were described as barbarians, ignorant of the culture of Rome and devoted to the gods of the north.

In A.D. 874, the Danish army broke into two parts and began to turn from military conquest towards permanent settlement of the lands it had conquered. One part under its leader Halfden moved north as far as the Tyne and, after a year spent in harrying the Picts and Strathclyde Celts, it returned to the area south of the Tees. By the River Swale and in what is now North Yorkshire the Danes then began to settle down making their homes and beginning to farm the land. The number of place names of Danish origin in this part of Yorkshire is an indication of the extent of Danish settlement.

These Danish settlers had been established for little more than one generation before the area was threatened by other Scandinavian intruders. Of the Norsemen who came to

England from Ireland and the Isle of Man some settled in the North West, others crossed the Pennines, some into Swaledale but many moving eastwards into the areas inhabited by the Danes.Though closely akin, Norsemen and Danes were not necessarily well disposed to one another and in the first half of the 10th century the Norsemen sought to gain control of York and all the Danish settlements in Yorkshire.They succeeded but York was eventually retaken by Athelstan, grandson of Alfred the Great. In the year 937, Athelstan moved with his army through Catterick and went northwards to meet a combined force of Irish Norsemen and the Scots of Strathclyde who had been invading English territory. At the battle of Brunanburgh which followed, the English won a decisive victory.

It was in 947 that perhaps the most famous Viking leader of his time, 'Eric Bloodaxe' arrived in Northumbria and the Norsemen who had settled there immediately hailed him as their King. For two years, Eric 'reigned' in York in defiance of the Irish Norsemen as well as the Danes and English but in 954, he is said to have been 'expelled' by the Northumbrians and the tradition is that he met his death on Stainmore at the hands of one Maccus, the son of Olaf Guthfrithson, the leader of the Irish Norsemen. The expulsion and subsequent death of Eric Bloodaxe marked the end of the Scandinavian attempt to establish an independent kingdom based on Dublin and York and the people of the Swale and of Northumbria were henceforward governed by a succession of earls ruling nominally as deputies of the kings of England.

With the rest of Northumbria, the country of the River Swale south of Richmond had been invaded by the Danes and the Norsemen. At one time there seemed to be a possibility of a permanent Scandinavian state being established to include the whole area north of the Humber as well as the stronghold in Ireland. The fall of Eric Bloodaxe and differences that emerged between the Danes and the Norsemen ensured that such an arrangement would fail and in the end, it was the power of the English monarchy that prevailed to govern the country.

Though there have been many Viking findings in York, the Scandinavians generally left little archaeological evidence as compared with the Anglo-Saxons. This is sometimes attributed to the fact that the Danes and Norsemen who settled around the Swale and elsewhere adopted the Christian faith and discarded heathen burials. The main evidence of their settlement is derived from place names. Many Scandinavian names are common to both Danes and Norseman and perhaps the most familiar are those which include 'by', meaning a village. Apart from Skeeby and Easby mentioned earlier, there are Maundby, Gatenby, Baldersby, Helperby and Killerby. There are many other Scandinavian elements but some, like 'thorpe' meaning a hamlet are peculiar to the Danes. Other names, like 'gill' are specifically Norse.

The language of the Scandinavians continued to be used in Britain until at least the 11th century and, even today, Norwegians visiting Upper Swaledale hear words they can understand in the dialect of the older people.

CHAPTER XIII

Castle Hills, Henry Jenkins of Ellerton, the Scorton Cursus and Kiplin Hall

BY THE RIVER SWALE BELOW Catterick is the ancient stronghold of Castle Hill. This has been described as an earthen mound in the shape of a parallelogram and enclosed by a ditch. The site has yielded some interesting historical remains and, though Clarkson links it with the Roman occupation, there is also evidence of Anglian burials nearby and little doubt that the site served as a British or Anglian settlement being also used at the time of the Danish intrusions.

At nearby Killerby a Castle was built in later years and was granted by the first Earl of Richmond to Scollandus of Bedale. Subsequently, it became the principal residence of Brian Fitz-Alan. When the antiquarian Leland visited the area in the middle of the 16th century however, he reported that the Castle was in ruins. Though little remains of the Castle today,the probable site is occupied by the imposing Killerby Hall, a Jacobean building of brick with stone quoins. A short distance away is the late 18th century Kirkby Hall and the Church of St Mary of Kirkby Fleetham. The village of Kirkby was mentioned in the Domesday Book as 'Cherchebi'and local opinion suggests that the Church which has a Norman doorway may have been

34. *Killerby Hall.*

rebuilt in the 11th century from an original wooden structure. Of particular interest in the Church is a fine effigy of a fully mailed Knight Templar.

Looking across the River from Killerby, one can see the village of Ellerton-on-Swale. It comprises the two hamlets of North and South Ellerton, where there is a late 17th century Manor House. Ellerton's main claim to fame is that it was the home of Henry Jenkins, an extraordinary man who is reputed to have lived to the great age of 169 years. Though such a long life is difficult to believe, there is in fact considerable weight of evidence to confirm that Henry Jenkins' life spanned an extensive period of English history. He is said to have been born in the year 1500 and died at Ellerton in 1670. He could neither read nor write and when asked how he earned a living, he replied 'salmon fishing and thatching cottages'.

35. *An impression of the long lived Henry Jenkins.*
(WITH ACKNOWLEDGEMENT TO THE RICHMONDSHIRE MUSEUM)

Those who wrote of his life recall that, at the time of the Battle of Flodden, when he was only 12 years old, he was sent to Northallerton with a horse-drawn load of arrows for the army of the Earl of Surrey on its march north. He had a vivid recollection of the dissolution of the monasteries in 1536 and in 1667 he gave evidence in Court in a case involving the Vicar of Catterick and a landowner. Later, in another case in York Jenkins was said to be aged 140 years old.

This amazing man swam in the Swale when he was over 100 and it is evident that he retained his sight and hearing until his death. Indeed, his sight was good enough to enable him to tie his own fishing flies, even in his later years. Henry Jenkins was born before parish records were kept but the entry for his burial at Bolton-on-Swale on 9th December 1670 records that he was 'a very aged and poore man of Ellerton'. There is a marble tablet on the south wall of the chancel in Bolton's Church of St Mary commemorating his life.

This Parish Church of St Mary was built on the site of previous structures, Norman and Anglian, and the remains of both are seen incorporated with the Church's more recent Gothic style. The present Church was built by the brethren of St Mary of York who owned large tracts of land in the area. The initial work began in the first half of the 14th century but the building was later enlarged, Victorianised and restored in 1859. Near the Church of St Mary and occupying a typical manorial position is Bolton Old Hall which is a 15th century tower house built by a branch of the important Scrope family.

A short distance from Bolton is the village of Scorton with its purpose built Grammar School dating back to 1760; an interesting building which is sadly no longer in use as a school. Of special historical importance has been the discovery of the Scorton Cursus — or course — which is considered to date back to the late Neolithic period. It is a site discovered by Professor J.K. St Joseph in 1949. It was located on the terraces of the old

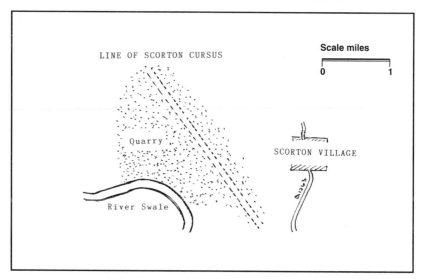

36. *The location of Scorton Cursus.*

river gravels of the Swale and excavation was undertaken across a section of the Cursus in advance of gravel extraction. Much evidence had already been destroyed but it was possible to trace the outline of the Cursus, which had a length of at least two kilometres. There were two main very straight ditches on either side of the length and a traverse at the south-eastern end. To the west of the Cursus there was a single primary burial with a beaker and evident outline of a coffin. The Cursus may have had some religious significance and the possibility is that it was used on neolithic ceremonial occasions.

Only a short journey down-River from Ellerton is Kiplin Hall and it is there that the story needs to be told of the Calverts. In 1580, a Leonard Calvert of Danby Wiske married a local girl, Alice Crossland. They were Catholics and came to live in Kiplin as tenants in a Tudor house built by Lord Scrope after the Reformation. Leonard and his wife had a son they named George who proved to be endowed with 'singular gifts of mind, candour, integrity and prudence'. He took his B.A. at Trinity College, Oxford and then studied law at Lincoln's Inn from 1598 to 1601. His career led him to the Court of James I and later to the post of Junior Secretary to Sir Robert Cecil, who became the Earl of Salisbury. At the age of forty, George Calvert followed in Salisbury's footsteps and became Principal Secretary to James I with particular concern for foreign affairs. He was knighted and later became Lord Baltimore with large grants of land in Ireland — though there is no evidence that he ever visited that country.

George Calvert had earlier married Ann, the daughter of George Myms and they had no less than ten children. Of these, the two most notable were the eldest sons Cecil and Leonard. Having achieved a well paid position, George was able to buy the estate property at Kiplin and he resolved to build the Kiplin Hall that stands by the River Swale today. It was probably completed about 1625 and is an interesting symmetrical

37. Kiplin Hall.

building which draws on features from Italy or France but seems very basically English. Said to be built from designs by Inigo Jones, the Hall stands in attractive parkland on the east side of the River Swale.

George Calvert's wife died in 1622 and, in 1625, only six years after achieving his high office, he resigned his position. Reaffirming his Catholic faith, he decided to turn his attention to affairs beyond the confines of Europe. He had received a grant of land in Ireland and was created Baron Baltimore presumably after the Irish port in County Cork.This title was to prove very appropriate in his subsequent dealings with America. He spent a considerable amount of money setting up a colony in Newfoundland which he called Avalon but this proved a failure and he was obliged to abandon the project. Eventually King Charles I granted him land to the north of the Potomac River in eastern America and there a colony was established. It prospered and was named Maryland in honour of Charles I's consort Queen Maria.

Sadly however, George Calvert the 1st Lord Baltimore, died in 1632, before the grant of the colony was finally completed and it was made in favour of his eldest son Cecil, the 2nd Lord Baltimore. The rent for the whole colony was given as two Indian arrows and one fifth of all the gold and silver discovered.

Cecil, like his father, was a remarkable man. With his brother Leonard as governor, he administered Maryland with admirable competence and foresight, all apparently without setting foot in the colony. Yet he clearly placed much reliance on Leonard who had sailed to the colony in the 'Ark and Dove' in 1634 with another brother George and some two hundred other settlers. Today, in the Public Library of Baltimore hang the pictures of the founder and five generations of proprietors of the successful colony of Maryland, surely a tribute to George Calvert and the family which he founded.

CHAPTER XIV

The Rampaging Normans and the Domesday Survey

THERE WERE MANY PERIODS OF bitter conflict during the post-Roman invasions by the Anglo Saxons, the Danes and Norsemen, but few such episodes of those times can compare with the ruthless devastation of the Norman pillage of the Northumbrian country between the Humber and the River Tyne of which the hinterland of the River Swale was part. It could be argued in retrospect that William of Normandy had good reason for retribution but it is evident that, in later life, William himself was haunted by the bloodshed for which he was responsible.

The events which led up to this appalling massacre began with King Harold's defeat at the Battle of Hastings on 14th October 1066. William's victory made him master only of the south-east of England and gained little acceptance in the North or for that matter in the West of England or Wales. On the death of Harold, Morcar — who was Earl of Northumbria — his brother Edwin and other nobles, named Edgar Atheling as heir to the throne. The word Atheling means Royal Prince and Edgar was the grandson of Edmund Ironside. However, the Norman invasion of England had been given Pope Alexander's blessing and despite the opposition, the Clergy and Church were universally in favour of the conquering Duke William being made King. Their wishes were granted and William of Normandy was indeed crowned King of England by Aldred, Archbishop of York on Christmas Day, 1066.

Morcar and his brother Edwin were at first persuaded to acknowledge the new King but they were soon to find that William made abundant promises which he failed to fulfil and they turned against him. It also became clear that Northumbria was unwilling to acknowledge William's authority and in 1068, Morcar and Edwin led an uprising which was supported by Gospatric, Earl of Bernicia.They marshalled their forces to confront the Normans and York became the centre for the uprising.

William was soon told of the build-up of opposition forces and he quickly gathered an army together and marched to York. Morcar and Edwin appear to have been taken by surprise and they were forced to yield and disband their troops. Many were imprisoned and Earl Gospatrick with Edgar Atheling, the would-be heir to the throne, fled to Scotland.Though William then returned to the south, seemingly well pleased with his expedition, he was soon to be made aware that Northumbria was not yet conquered.

Within twelve months there was a further uprising. In January 1069, the King gave Robert of Comines the Earldom of Northumbria to replace Gospatrick and sent him to occupy his Earldom. Robert of Comines went to Durham but, according to the Anglo-Saxon Chronicle, he was soon attacked and burned to death in the Bishop's Palace, many of his Norman followers being massacred. This was promptly followed by a spontaneous rising in York where Robert FitzRichard, one of William's appointed commanders of the garrison, was slain together with many of his guards.

King William was angered by these events and again responded quickly by moving north with his troops to York, taking the rebels by surprise. They were routed and William slew several hundreds of those who could not escape. He then handed the city over to the plunder of his soldiers and sent a force of his men to Durham with instructions to avenge the death of Robert of Comines. However, there was a heavy mist in the area and, much to the relief of the rebels, William's men, having lost their way, returned to York without reaching their goal.

The restless North again rose in rebellion in the autumn of 1069. Morcar and his brother with Edgar and Gospatric had sought help both from the Scots and from Denmark. The arrival in Northumbria of Osbern, brother of the Danish King, was therefore welcomed. In September, a fleet of 240 Danish ships sailed up the Humber to help the English cause and their arrival was the signal for the third and greatest rising against William. Several thousand men from Scotland joined with the Northumbrians and marched to York. With them was Gospatrick and another of William's enemies, Waltheof the Earl of Huntingdon. Edgar Atheling sailed down from Scotland to join with the Danes.

So it was that a considerable force of William's enemies banded together and marched on York. The defensive castles William had built there were soon overwhelmed and a great many Normans are said to have been slain. After the attack, the rebel troops retreated with the booty they had taken, and the Danes returned to their ships. A formidable figure in this attack had been The Earl Waltheof and he remained in York with a supporting English garrison.

When York fell, William was busy quelling a revolt in Devonshire and he was also having trouble with the Welsh who were besieging Shrewsbury. There seems little doubt that if all the rebels in the country had united at that time against the Normans, history would have been different.

William was so enraged with the news of the attack on York that he vowed he would ravage Northumbria and destroy its people. With a large army he went to York and laid siege to the English garrison. Waltheof defended himself with skill and resolution and withstood the Norman attack, only yielding when famine compelled him to do so. Strangely, King William saw fit not only to pardon Waltheof but to make him Earl of Northumbria.

What happened next was not an act of plunder but simple unmitigated devastation. With appalling ferocity, William and his army gradually moved through Northumbria slaughtering the people and laying waste the whole countryside. Few villages between York and Durham were left inhabited and many thousands of people perished in the area either by the sword or through famine. Cattle were slain, houses and crops burned, fields ravaged and food destroyed. The Vale of York suffered terribly and the hand of William fell heaviest on the lands of those who had led the rebels like Edwin and Gospatric. It was one of the most ruthless acts of destruction in our early history, and the responsibility lay entirely with the King whose army acted under his direct orders.

The people living in many of the villages by the River Swale suffered dreadfully. Those who were able to escape death fled wherever they could, some into the higher parts of the Dales and others are thought to have found their way to Scotland. With little or no food however, many did not survive and for nine or more years many parts of the region were said to lie almost uninhabited and desolate.

The land that William the Conqueror had taken over already possessed a highly developed territorial organisation. England south of the River Tees was completely divided into shires which were again divided into wapentakes and then vills. In 1086, William ordered a thorough investigation into the wealth of the whole country. He sent his men into every shire to make a comprehensive record of land and property and to ascertain the exact value of each area and estate in the country so that he could levy the taxes he needed to pay for the occupation.

He wanted to know the number of taxable carucates and ploughs that were available to him and how much land and livestock he owned as King. It was a survey carried out efficiently and with surprising speed and the information collected was recorded in the appropriately named Domesday Book. Apart from providing William with the detailed information he sought, the results of the survey have proved to be of great historical value to us today. There are in fact a number of ways in which William's methods of government and administration have benefited us today.

Despite the time which had elapsed since the appalling destruction of Northumbrian life, the Domesday survey provided us with a reminder of the extent of the Norman devastation in the area of the River Swale and elsewhere. In Catterick and in the hinterland of the River to the south, it was evident that in the years following the Northumbrian invasion the Norman landowners had repaired some of the earlier ravages but higher up the Swale many villages had seemingly ceased to exist. A village like Reeth was recorded as having six carucates taxable and three ploughs possible but nevertheless the land was reported to be waste. Similar reports were recorded about other villages like Fremington, Grinton, Ellerton, Marrick and Downholme, the place called Hindrelag, as well as Hudswell and Scotton where in each case there was only waste land available.

It must be said however that when a village or holding was declared 'waste' it was not necessarily devoid of resources but the term seemed to convey that there was no population. The Domesday survey gave the impression that people from the 'waste' villages who had sought safety elsewhere had not returned in any number by the year 1086. It is possible that some of those who sought refuge in the high parts of Swaledale may have remained after integrating with earlier settlers. There is also some evidence that local people were moved by their landlords to estates in other areas and this may have prevented or delayed a return to their original villages.

In the year 1087 William the Conqueror died at the Priory of Saint Gervais outside Rouen in France. In his last moments his thoughts went to his conquest of England 'achieved at a terrible cost out of all proportion to the benefits that it conferred'. Before he died he is reputed to have said...

"I persecuted the native inhabitants of England beyond all reason. Whether nobles or commons, I cruelly oppressed them; many I unjustly disinherited; innumerable multitudes, especially in the county of York, perished through me by famine and sword.... I am stained with the rivers of blood that I have shed."

CHAPTER XV

William the Conqueror's Land Divisions and the Country of the Lower Swale

BEFORE THE NORMAN CONQUEST, an Anglo-Scandinavian aristocracy had built up in England but William replaced this with Norman-French tenants-in-chief who together with the King held all the territorial wealth of the country. By the end of his reign however, it was apparent that William actually owned very little and a high proportion of the land was in the ownership of mainly rich Norman or Breton families many of whom also had land in France. These families created a new form of aristocracy.

William divided the land into units known as honours which varied in size but some of which were large and widely dispersed. These units were created for military purposes and each lord of an honour had to undertake to furnish the King with a specified number of mounted and armed cavalrymen whenever he wanted them for military duty at home or abroad. The honours were divisible into manors which the lord in possession could either cultivate himself as demesne land or let to tenants in return for rent and services.

Earl Alan had been in charge of the Breton contingent at Hastings and, as described in Chapter 6, he was granted the

Honour of Richmond, a huge estate which included much of Swaledale. It was in fact one of the three largest feudal holdings granted by William. As already mentioned, this like other such divisions, was created mainly to establish military control over the area and Earl Alan built his Castle at Richmond as a centre from which he could govern and maintain control. The Honour of Richmond continued to be held by the Earl and his descendants over nearly three centuries until the reign of Henry IV, when it was granted to Ralph Neville.

There were a number of manorial divisions of the land in Swaledale but the Manor of Healaugh was the largest, occupying the whole of the main valley from Grinton and Fremington westwards, an area of 52,000 acres. Earl Alan's estate however continued down the Swale far beyond Richmond and Catterick until ultimately, the River flows into the former estate of another great landowner, William de Percy.

38. *Langton Hall.*

As the River leaves Catterick, the centre of so much early history, it begins to move southwards and winds its way like the coils of a snake through the more fertile lands leading to the Vale of York. After passing Kiplin the Swale reaches Great and Little Langton both of which are named in the Domesday Book. Overlooking the River from the east bank stands the imposing building of Langton Hall. Originally called Langton Lodge, it was built about 1770 by Leonard Smelt. He was the son of William Smelt, owner of the manor of Little Langton and Member of Parliament for Northallerton in 1740, a seat which he resigned on his appointment as Receiver General of Revenues on the island of Barbados.

In 1851, the property was bought by Lord Teignmouth and after extensions and alterations in the Gothic style, it was named Langton Hall. In more recent times, the present owner Major W.A. Fife asked the architect Sir Martyn Beckett to draw plans which as far as possible would return the property to its original size and character. This work was completed in 1961 and Lord Teignmouth's Gothic additions — more than fourteen rooms — were removed.

The Scandinavian and particularly the Danish occupation period is evidenced by the names of several villages in the area of the Lower Swale. Thrintoft, originally a Danish settlement, is reached some two miles down River from Langton Hall. Here in a local farmyard is a small but historic rectangular building which was originally the Chapel of St Mary Magdalene. Though the existing building, now being used as a barn, is thought to be 15th century, the origins of the Chapel have been traced back to the middle of the 13th century when a grant of land in the village enabled a Picot de Lascelles to found a Chantry Chapel which was connected with Jervaulx Abbey. Picot de Lascelles was the son of Roger Lascelles, Lord of Scruton. Records indicate that a chaplain was appointed to enable divine service to be celebrated regularly in this little Thrintoft Chapel.

The history of the village of Scruton, which stands on the opposite bank of the Swale, certainly goes back to the 6th or 7th century Anglian period. The village is remembered today as the birthplace of the Gales, a much respected family of antiquarians. It was in 1688 that Thomas Gale purchased the Manor of Scruton. He married a relation of Samuel Pepys, the diarist, became Headmaster of St Paul's School in London, Regius Professor of Greek at Cambridge University and a respected Dean of York. He was buried in York Minster where there is a memorial stone. Thomas was followed by Roger Gale who built Scruton Hall about 1705 and became a Fellow of Trinity College, Cambridge as well as the Treasurer to the Royal Society. His main literary work was the 'Registrum Honoris de Richmond' written in 1722. Roger had a brother Samuel who was also a recognised antiquarian.

39. *Scruton Hall – originally the home of the Gales family. The hall was demolished in 1958.*
(PHOTOGRAPH BY PERMISSION OF THE NORTHERN ECHO)

Scruton Hall was originally an attractive Queen Anne house to which wings were added resulting in a building of some grandeur. In 1795 the direct male line of the Gales died out and the manor of Scruton passed to the Coore family. A member of that family, the Reverend Alfred Coore, served in India as a missionary and later became a great designer and builder of churches mostly in Hindu and Mogul styles. He designed no less than fifty churches, schools and other buildings though he was self-taught and never qualified as an architect. The Hall was sold in 1953 and, to the regret of the local villagers, it was demolished in 1958. The oldest building now standing in Scruton is the Church, the history of which dates back to the 13th century though it was largely rebuilt in 1856 by the Coore family.

Leaving Scruton, the River passes Morton on Swale with its substantial stone bridge built by John Carr about 1800. According to Leland this must have replaced an earlier wooden structure. Near the bridge, the original Morton Hall, now occupied as a farmhouse, had a windmill and a communal oven. A short distance from Morton is the Domesday village of Ainderby Steeple dominated by its Parish Church of St Helen. After the Norman Conquest the patronage of this church and the surrounding land was tenanted to one of Earl Alan's followers named Anschitel, and later in the 14th century these interests were acquired by Geoffrey de Scrope. In 1458 the patronage of the church was granted by the Scrope family to the Abbot and convent of Jervaulx and remained under them until the Dissolution.

As the Swale meanders on through good fertile farming land, it passes Gatenby where there is an interesting 17th century building known earlier as the Ivy Garth Cottages. Here regular Church services were once held, conducted by the Vicar of nearby Burneston. In coaching days Gatenby is believed to have been a well known stopping place with two inns known

40. *Allerthorpe Hall.*

as the Oak Tree and the New Inn. A short distance away is the impressive 17th century Allerthorpe Hall with its two fine chimney stacks and a gabled central porch. Records indicate that in 1550, Sir Thomas Lascelles Kt. conveyed the local manor to William Robinson and when the Hall was built in 1608 it remained in the hands of the Robinson family until quite recent times. Though no trace now remains, it is known that in the monastic period there was a Priory here at Allerthorpe for the canons of the Premonstratensian order; the canons of this order were located at Easby Abbey. After only a short period however, the Priory was moved to Coverham.

Allerthorpe Hall has historical links with the ancient perpendicular style Church of St Lambert at Burneston. St Lambert was Bishop of Maastricht and was martyred in 705 A.D. The church was first mentioned in 1089 when it was given with four carucates of land to the monks of the Abbey of St Mary, York. However, work on the present building did not

112

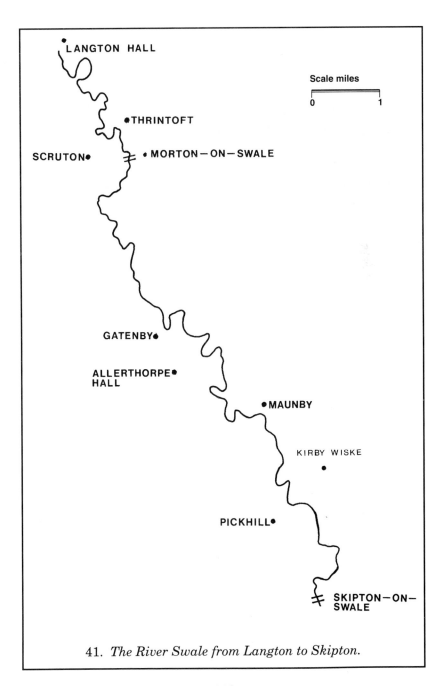

41. *The River Swale from Langton to Skipton.*

113

begin until 1390 and was not completed for two hundred years. In 1627, Thomas Robinson of Allerthorpe Hall donated a complete set of carved oak pews to the Church and in 1680, another Robinson — Matthew — who was then Vicar of Burneston, founded some almshouses in the village which are still in use today. It is of no small interest to followers of lawn tennis that a later Vicar of Burneston, the Reverend J.T. Hartley, won the Wimbledon Men's Singles Championship in 1879 and 1880. He was the first and probably the last practising clergyman to win this Championship.

Continuing down river east of the Swale, Maunby is another village having Danish origins, its name meaning a boundary pillar or cairn of stones. Here there is an imposing 18th century mansion house with picturesque gardens and a double line of linden trees in its frontage. The village of Kirby Wiske is a short distance away as are Sion Hall and Danotty Hall. The original Sion Hall dates back to the 18th century and passed

42. *The Burneston Almshouses.*

114

into the hands of the Hon. George Lascelles before being sold in 1911 when it was demolished and rebuilt to the designs of Walter Brierley.

The nearby Danotty Hall can claim to have a particularly interesting history. It is known to have been purchased in the 17th century by a Daniel Auty, formerly a Leeds clothier. He was described as 'waxing rich' and suspicions that he was engaged in illegal doings proved to be well founded. He was an expert forger of coins and there were secret rooms fitted out in the Hall for this purpose. Auty had a daughter who married a man named Busby who was admitted as a partner in the illegal forgery business. However, disputes arose between the two partners and Busby killed his father in law. He was executed for his crime and no doubt the existence of the forgery business then came to light.

Further to the south is Breckenbrough Hall which was originally described as a castellated mansion which, according to Camden, became known as the seat of the Lascelles family. The Hall was rebuilt in 1894, and has recently been occupied by a school. Across the River is Pickhill, which is dominated by its Church of All Saints dating back at least to the 12th century with restoration in the late 19th century by G.E. Street. The Church has a beautiful Norman doorway and arch leading to the chancel. There is now no trace of Pickhill Castle, once the home of Sir Andrew Neville.

Passing Skipton on Swale and the village of Catton, the River reaches Baldersby St James and the rich pastures of Baldersby Park. Here a Georgian mansion was built by Sir William Robinson in 1658 and it became known as Newby Hall. About 1840 the ownership passed to George Hudson, described in his time as 'The Railway King'. His involvement in the development of Yorkshire railways was considerable and the importance of York as a railway centre has been largely attributed to his foresight and skill.

The history of the Manor of Topcliffe goes back at least to Anglian times and in the Domesday Book the village is referred to as 'Topeclive'. The survey made clear how much the village had suffered from the Norman intrusion but, following the Conquest, this and several other manors were given to William de Percy as a reward for his valour at the Battle of Hastings. The Percys established themselves in a large mott and bailey castle built on what is now known as Maiden Bower, an artificial mound on a tongue of land between the Swale and its tributary Colbeck. This remained their principal residence until the early part of the 14th century when Henry de Percy purchased the barony and castle at Alnwick in Northumberland. However the great Earls of Northumberland, as they became known, maintained their links with Topcliffe which became a market town of considerable importance.

The history of the ancient Percy family provides an extraordinary record of war and bloodshed. At least six of the Percy earls died violent deaths. Henry the 1st Earl was killed at the Battle of Bramham Moor in 1408, Henry the 2nd died at the Battle of St Albans, and Henry the 3rd was slain at the Battle of Towton. Henry the 4th was killed by a mob at Topcliffe following the imposition of a land tax and, of the other casualties, Thomas the 7th Earl was beheaded at York and Henry the 9th shot himself in the Tower of London. A similar fate befell Thomas Percy, brother of the 1st Earl who was beheaded in 1403 and this record of deaths in battle or by other means continued into later generations.

The killing of Henry the 4th Earl in Topcliffe calls for particular mention because of the scale of his subsequent funeral. Parliament had granted Henry VII a subsidy for carrying on the war in Brittany. The country was already impoverished however by the long struggle between the houses of York and Lancaster and when a new land tax was imposed there was violent opposition particularly by the people of the northern counties, and especially Yorkshire. It was the duty of Henry the 4th Earl as Lord Lieutenant to enforce the payment but, at Topcliffe, the people broke into the Manor House and murdered the Earl and many of his servants. The funeral which followed reached an extraordinary scale of magnificence. The hearse set out from Topcliffe for Beverley followed by twelve lords, twenty gentlewomen, squires, yeomen and a host of mourners said to 'extend for miles' in solemn and gorgeous pageantry. The funeral procession spent two nights on its way and when it eventually reached Beverley, requiem mass was sung and the body deposited in the Percy chantry.

A church is said to have been built in Topcliffe between the 6th and 7th centuries but the first stone built church was erected by William de Percy in 1066.On the site today is the historic Church of St Columbus and here is found the great brass of Thomas of Topcliffe and his wife Mabel, one of the finest brass engravings in the country. It dates back to the year 1391 and a design found on the back of the engraving is dated 1335. The Topcliffes were an ancient family in the area and, by intermarriage, they became allied to the Percys. However, there is little else to remind us of the Topcliffes or the presence of the great Percy family. The castle which was their stronghold has long gone and the only trace remaining is the site at Maiden Bower, which was encompassed by a moat some of which is still visible.

CHAPTER XVI

Eldmire, Cundall, Paulinus at Brafferton, and the Battle of Myton

AS THE SWALE TWISTS AND turns on its way southwards, it passes the abandoned village of Eldmire (or Elmire). The village was first recorded in 1236 and it was mentioned again in 1327 and 1334 being linked with nearby Crakehill. In 1338 a chantry

43. Cundall Hall.

Chapel of St Giles was established in Eldmire bringing to mind a possible connection with the Hospital of St Giles referred to in chapter 8. The site of the Chapel was subsequently occupied by Eldmire Farm which was demolished in more recent times. From aerial surveys the outline of the village and of two integrated fishponds can be seen. It seems likely that the village suffered considerably from the Scottish raids though its abandonment could well have resulted from constant flooding from the River.

The history of Cundall, on the west bank of the River, appears to go back well before the time of the Domesday Survey. By the end of the 16th century, the Manor of Cundall had changed hands a number of times but when the ownership passed to Robert Walters in 1597 it was to remain in his family for several generations. Indeed, the Walters family became closely linked not only with Cundall but also with the City of York.

Robert Walters became Lord Mayor of York on two occasions. Firstly in 1591 in the reign of Elizabeth I and again in 1603 at the time of James I by whom Robert was knighted. William Walters, brother and heir of Sir Robert was also Lord Mayor of York in 1620. His son Christopher married Dorothy, the daughter of Sir Robert Strickland and their grandson Robert kept the family name to the fore by becoming the High Sheriff of the County of York in 1660.

Records show that there was a windmill as well as a water mill in Cundall in the 16th and 17th centuries and the 19th century Church of St Mary and All Saints is adjacent to the site of a much earlier church probably built in the 14th century. Today, the 17th century Cundall Hall with its ancient barn stands high on the slopes above the village overlooking the River Swale below, and serves to remind us of the important role played by generations of the Cundall family of Walters.

The writings of the Venerable Bede and others make it clear that Paulinus travelled widely in the North-East preaching and converting the people to Christianity. The visits by Paulinus to Bernicia as well as East Anglia and his considerable work in the area of the River Swale at Catterick have already been described as has Camden's description of baptisms in the Swale at Brafferton two miles south of Cundall. Paulinus had begun by baptising at Brafferton in a local well but this ran dry and the Bishop then continued to baptise in the River. The Church of St Peter at Brafferton is close to the River bank and is believed to stand on the very spot where Paulinus preached Christianity to the assembled people.

At the village of Myton, the River is near to the end of its journey, but the village and the land nearby are particularly interesting to historians. Like so many other villages, Myton was declared 'waste' when the Domesday survey was undertaken. As it revived, the Church of St Mary was built using materials brought from the Roman town of Isurium or Aldborough, close to Boroughbridge.

The family of Stapeltons — or Stapyltons — was of considerable importance in the River Swale area over many centuries. The family name is derived from the village of Stapleton near Darlington, which in Anglian times was an important trading point being located on the border between Deira and Bernicia. The pedigree of the family appears to start in 1176 with Nicholas de Stapelton or "Filius Galfridi", as he was described in a charter of Jervaulx Abbey. Nicholas became Governor of Middleham Castle in 1216 and the records of his family show that he gave five oxgangs of land in Marske by the Swale to the monks of Jervaulx Abbey. An oxgang or bovate was as much land as one ox could plough in a year and the Jervaulx Abbey monks must have received at least 50 acres and probably considerably more.

44. *Myton Hall, home of the Stapyltons.*

Of the several branches of the family which developed over the years, the Myton branch, spelling its name Stapylton, was to become one of the more important. Heading this branch was Brian Stapylton who is said to have purchased the Myton estate in 1615. It was his daughter Frances who, in 1651, married John Hutton of Marske, son and heir apparent of Matthew Hutton (see Chapter 5). Brian's grandson — Sir Brian Stapylton — is believed to have built the present Myton Hall in 1693.

It was during the monastic period that the village of Myton gained importance as a wool transit centre and it is of interest to recount how this wool trade developed. At the time of the Domesday survey it was evident that, despite the devastation of the Conquest, flocks of sheep had begun to build up on the demesne lands of some of the large manors. The early 12th century saw the beginning of the great monastic era and with it,

121

a considerable development in sheep farming by the Cistercian and other orders.

The Cistercians who came from a wool producing area of France had acquired considerable skill in the handling of sheep. From their monasteries at Rievaulx, Byland, Jervaulx and Fountains, they gradually built up great flocks of sheep and their trade in wool expanded rapidly. Despite their rules of self sufficiency, they had a great desire to increase and beautify their buildings and their wool sales provided the finance for building developments at Fountains and other abbeys in the 13th century. The Cistercians in particular however, came to be regarded as ruthless landlords often clearing land for profit though it involved the loss of village communities.

In the valley of the Swale there were also the Benedictines, the Gilbertines, and the Premonstratensians as well as the Augustinians of Bridlington who had grazing rights in Swaledale. Every order was involved in some way with sheep breeding and wool production. The big Cistercian monasteries further south were the main providers with their higher quality wool which appealed to Italian and other overseas buyers but quantities of wool passed through Richmond. As the town began to gain importance as a market and transit centre recognised routes developed for the transit of wool to the east coast ports. As already mentioned, a great deal of wool was exported through the Tyne or Tees, but there was also a well recognised route from Richmond by packhorse and small river boats to Myton and thence to York and the Humber.

There is an iron bridge crossing the Swale a little below Myton village. Originally, this was probably built of wood and, though seemingly of no great importance, it is a bridge which stood at the centre of one of the most gruesome battles of Northern history. In the year 1319, Edward II was engaged with his followers in the siege of Berwick. Not caring to relieve the garrison of that town by any other means, the Scottish leaders, the Earl of Murray and Lord James Douglas decided to create a diversion. They collected an army, said to number 15,000 men, crossed the Solway and moved down into Northern England pillaging and laying waste the countryside wherever they went. They reached Boroughbridge which they reduced to ashes and then pushed on to the gates of York.

The Scots had heard that the Queen was in York and they had planned to take her prisoner and to offer peace to King Edward only on their own terms using the Queen as hostage. However, a spy from the Scottish camp who had been sent into York was taken prisoner and, under duress, told of the Scottish plan. The Archbishop of York and others concerned about the Queen's welfare arranged for her to be taken to Nottingham.

In a bid to defend the City from the Scottish invaders, the Archbishop together with the Bishop of Ely then began recruiting as many people as possible. A 'hybrid' army, said to be of

45. *Myton Bridge – the focal point of a tragic battle.*

10,000 men was formed and it included many white robed churchmen and lay-men. They moved out of York to face the Scots and the two forces met on the 20th September, 1319 at Myton.

The Scots feigned a retreat as the English advanced but, having crossed the Myton bridge, the invaders lay in ambush and lit haystacks, the smoke from which was driven westwards, blinding the oncoming English. It was then that the Scots advanced and pinned the Archbishop's army into a corner. The English were disorganised and, showing no mercy, the Scots slaughtered some 3,000 men; others are believed to have drowned in the River Swale. There were many priests, monks, and other churchmen amongst the dead. After this terrible slaughter, it is easy to believe the legend that the waters of the Swale, as they joined the Ure, were stained with the blood of the battle.

The Lord Mayor of York Sir Nicholas Fleming was killed, others were taken prisoner, but the Archbishop and the Bishop of Ely were able to escape on horseback. When news of this horrific event reached the King he raised the siege of Berwick and hastened to prevent the return of the Scots. It was to no avail; the Earl of Murray and Lord Douglas returned to Scotland with their army using a different route, pillaging the countryside as they went but not meeting the King's army.

Today, as the waters of the Swale join with the Ure the scene is a peaceful one. The horrors of battle are almost forgotten and apart from the occasional walker and the fisherman with his rod and line few come to visit what was once the scene of such human destruction.

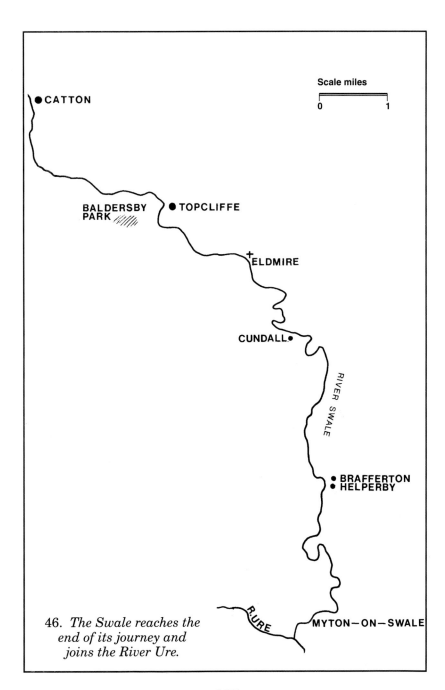

Scale miles

CATTON

BALDERSBY
PARK

TOPCLIFFE

ELDMIRE

CUNDALL

RIVER SWALE

BRAFFERTON
HELPERBY

R. URE

MYTON—ON—SWALE

46. *The Swale reaches the
end of its journey and
joins the River Ure.*

125

CHAPTER XVII

The End of the Journey

THOUGH THE BATTLE AT MYTON was probably one of the worst examples of Anglo-Scots conflict, the repeated incursions by the Scots, following the Battle of Bannockburn, brought fire and pillage to much of the River Swale country. Although Richmond, by paying large sums of money to the Scots on two occasions, suffered little from the raids, the surrounding areas were plundered mercilessly. In 1314 for instance, a Scottish army, having created much devastation in the area north of the Tees, moved south and plundered the country beyond Richmond before returning by Swaledale, burning, looting and driving away cattle. The ordinary farming folk of the area were the worst to suffer in this way but raids were frequently directed at monastic houses and it was in November 1347 that the Scots broke into Ellerton Priory and took away most of the few treasures it possessed.

The constant drain on resources caused by the Scottish intrusions seriously undermined the economic progress which had developed during the monastic era, and the 14th century was made the worse for the people of the River Swale by a series of plague epidemics. The 'Black Death' in 1349 and another epidemic in 1362 caused havoc particularly in Richmond which lost a considerable portion of its population. Though history may well have over emphasised the number of deaths, there seems little doubt that in Richmond alone the numbers who died from the plague exceeded 1,000 and the severity of the plague is emphasised by the need for a special plague cemetery at Easby.

The 15th century brought little respite from the agricultural stagnation, shortage of food and general poverty from which many ordinary people suffered particularly badly. When improvement ultimately came, it was gradual and was hindered by the reforms which followed the Dissolution of the monastic system and which were not universally accepted. For many local people, the Pilgrimage of Grace was just as much against poverty and social conditions as for any religious reasons. The passing of ex-monastic land and property to local landlords may have brought agricultural improvements but also increasing rents and inflation. Moreover, the custom of partible inheritance and the gradual fragmentation of tenancies led to uneconomic smallholdings and forced families to seek income from other sources. This particularly applied to the Dale above Reeth but in the more fertile agricultural areas of the lower Swale the problems of tenant farming do not appear to have been so evident.

The reign of Elizabeth I brought a period of comparative prosperity to the area of the Swale. The Queen did much to rejuvenate trade as well as showing concern for the welfare of her people. By encouraging the wearing of hand knitted stockings she created a change in fashion. From this, the hand knitting trade developed and almost every family in the Dale became involved. Payments were small but families came to regard knitting as a means of earning useful and often essential additional income. It continued over a period of some three centuries and has been revived in more recent times.

The development of the lead mining industry which can be traced back to Elizabeth's reign and came to the fore particularly in the 18th and 19th centuries not only changed the lives of a great many people already living by the Swale, it also brought a considerable increase in the population.

By the early 19th century the Swaledale population is estimated to have numbered about 7,500 people an increase of some 5,000 since the 16th century. Though conditions were far from good for the ordinary mining folk there was work to be had and the owners and officials were well rewarded. For some two centuries, the life of Swaledale became concentrated on the business of mining lead. Yet in mining there seems always to have been a day of reckoning when the mineral resources are depleted or production becomes cheaper elsewhere. With the import of cheaper lead from Spain it was the smaller less viable mines in Upper Swaledale which were the first to go. There was some revival in demand at the time of the Crimean War and a few mines continued to work into the 20th century. However, the important Old Gang Company finally went into liquidation in 1906 and other mines in Arkengarthdale which had made promising new discoveries were finally abandoned by 1912.

The end of the mining industry meant a return to hill farming for many of the Swaledale people who remained. Today the population is much reduced being swollen only by the numbers of visiting tourists. As the River reaches Richmond however and flows southwards to join the Ure, it passes through much richer farming countryside and rural communities of people who in the past have suffered greatly at the hands of invaders but have nevertheless played their role in this history of the holy River of St Paulinus.

Throughout the course of the River, the story of its people surely epitomises a continuous struggle for survival. The Romans, the Anglo-Saxons, the Scandinavians and the Normans have come and gone but perhaps their presence remains not only in the historical records but in the very character of many of those who live by the Swale today.

Bibliography

IN COMPILING THIS BOOK, I have been fortunate in being able to draw on the knowledge of local people whose families have lived by the River Swale for generations. I must also acknowledge the information provided by owners of some of the buildings and estates which have an important part to play in this history of the River Swale.

GENERAL REFERENCE BOOKS

A History of Richmond and Swaledale — Fieldhouse and Jennings (Phillimore 1978)

A New Historical Geography of England before 1600 — edited by H.C. Darby (Cambridge 1973, 1976)

A History of York and the North Riding — Whellan (Green 1871)

Early History of North Riding — Wm Edwards (Brown 1924)

Richmondshire Architecture — Jane Hatcher 1990

Bulmer's History and Directory of North Yorkshire — (Preston 1890)

The History of Richmondshire — T.D. Whitaker (Longman 1823)

Regal Richmondshire and the land of the Swale — Bogg (Elliott Stock 1909)

Romantic Richmondshire — Speight (Elliot Stock 1897)

The Victoria History of the Counties of England — Yorkshire North Riding edited by W. Page (Dawson 1968)

The History and Antiquities of Richmond — Clarkson (Bowman 1821)

Reference is also made to William Camden whose study 'Britannia' was translated into English in 1610 and to John Leland whose manuscripts relating to his tour of England are recorded in his 'Itinerary' of 1710.

PLACE NAMES

A Guide to the Anglo-Saxon Tongue — E.J. Vernon BA (Smith 1833)

Concise Oxford Dictionary of English Place Names — 7th edition 1977

Smith's Place Names of the North Riding of Yorkshire — Smith 1928

CHAPTER I

The Diaries of Lady Anne Clifford — 2nd edition (Sutton 1990)

Lady Anne Clifford — G.C. Williamson (Titus Wilson 1922)

Lady Anne's Way — Patrick Eyres (New Arcadians 1985)

Proud Northern Lady — Martyn Holmes (Phillimore 1975)

Swaledale — Ella Pontefract (Dent 1934)

Muker — The Story of a Yorkshire Parish (Chapter 4) — Edmund Cooper (Dalesman 1948)

The Dalesmen of the Mississippi River (page 114) — David Morris (Sessions 1989)

CHAPTER II

History of Lead Mining in the Pennines — Raistrick and Jennings (London 1965)

Roads and Trackways of The Yorkshire Dales — Wright (Morland Publishing 1985)

Muker — The Story of a Yorkshire Parish — Cooper (Dalesman 1948)

The History of Muker Church — E.R. Fawcett 1937

The Sixteenth Century Muker Communion Cup and its Maker — T.P. Cooper

CHAPTER III

Gunnerside Chapel and Gunnerside Folk — M. Batty (Teesdale 1967)

The Travelling Preacher — Geoffrey Milburn (Wesley Historical Society 1967)

Lead Mining and Smelting in Swaledale and Teesdale (Cleveland Industrial Archaeology Society Research Report No. 2)

Documents relating to the Swaledale Estates of Lord Wharton in the 16th/17th centuries. NYCC, April 1984

CHAPTER IV

Early Land Division and Settlement in Swaledale — T.C. Laurie (BAR 143 Chapter 8 1985)

Swaledale Ancient Land Boundaries Project — Survey Reports 1984-91 — Andrew Fleming and Tim Laurie

The Character of the Country — edited by Loren N. Horton (Iowa State Historical Department 1976)

Bygone Reeth — M. Batty (Reeth Methodist Church Council 1985)

The Draycott Hall Manuscripts Vols. 1-2-3. (North Riding County Council 1975)

CHAPTER V

Ruined Abbeys of Yorkshire — W.C. Lefroy Seeley 1911

Yorkshire Abbeys and the Wool Trade — H.E. Wroot (Thoresby Society 1930)

Man on a Donkey — H.M. Prescot (Eyre and Spottiswood 1952)

Marske in Swaledale — J. Raine (Bradbury Raine 1880)

Ebor — The Archbishops of York — A. Tindall Hart (Sessions 1986)

CHAPTER VI

Richmond Castle (in Richmond Castle and Easby Abbey) — John Weaver (English Heritage 1989)

Domesday Book — Yorkshire Parts 1 and 2 (History from the Sources) General Editor John Morris (Phillimore 1986)

The Culloden Tower and the Yorke Family — Privately printed in conjunction with the Landmark Trust

CHAPTER VII

The Corn Mills of Richmond — C.J. Hatcher and Billy Bank Copper Mine — L.P. Wenham, both in 'A Richmond Miscellany' (N.R. Record Office Publication No. 24 1980)

Yorkshire Woollen and Worsted Industries — Heaton (Oxford 1965)

Studies in English Trade in the 15th century — Power and Poston (Cambridge 1932)

The Wool Trade in English Medieval History — E. Power (Oxford 1941)

The English Stocking Knitting Industry 1500-1700 — Joan Thirsk (From the Textile and Economic History — Essays in Honour of Miss Julia Lucy Mann)

The Old Hand Knitters of the Dales — Hartley and Ingleby (Galava 1951)

CHAPTER VIII

Easby Abbey (in Richmond Castle and Easby Abbey) — John Weaver (English Heritage 1989)

St Giles Hospital — Archaeological Excavations — Peter Cardwell (1990)

The Burghs of Brough Hall — Pollard (N.Y.C.C 1980)

Documents re Chapel of St Ann, Catterick Bridge Y.A.J. 20/218

CHAPTER IX

Recent Work at Catterick — P.R. Wilson (From Settlement and Society in the Roman North edited by P.R. Wilson and D.M. Evans 1984)

Cataractonium — Fort and Town — E.J.W. Hillyard (Y.A.J. Vol. 39 pp. 224/5)

Yorkshire Towns in the Fourth Century — J.S. Wacher (from Soldier and Civilian in Roman Yorkshire 1971)

CHAPTER X

Bede's Ecclesiastical History of England — Revised Translation — A.M. Sellar (Bell 1912)

Bede's History of the English Nation — Plummer (Oxford 1896)

The Ecclesiastical History of the English Nation — Everyman's Library No. 479 (Dent 1958)

The World of Bede — Peter Hunter Blair (Sack & Warburg 1970)

An Introduction to Anglo-Saxon England — Peter Hunter Blair (Cambridge 1956)

The Origins of Northumbria — Peter Hunter Blair (Northumberland Press 1948)

Anglo-Saxon England — Peter Hunter Blair (Cambridge 1976)

Anglo-Saxon England — Sir Frank Stenton (Oxford 1971)

The History and Antiquities of Cleveland — J. Ward (Simpkin and Marshall 1846)

CHAPTER XI

Paulinus — F.W. Faber (Faber 1844)

Lives of the English Saints — Bishop of Worcester (Toovey 1844)

CHAPTER XII

Bede's Ecclesiastical History of England — Revised Translation — A.M. Sellar (Bell 1912)

The Ecclesiatical History of the English Nation — Everyman's Library No. 479 (Dent 1958)

Anglo-Saxon England (Chapter VIII) — Sir Frank Stenton (Oxford 1971)

Vikings, Angles and Danes in Yorkshire — A. Raistrick (Dalesman 1965)

The Anglo-Scandinavian Foundations — H.C. Darby (in the New Historical Geography of England before 1600) (Cambridge 1973)

CHAPTER XIII

Evidences of the Great Age of Henry Jenkins — John Bell (Richmond 1859)

Scorton Cursus — Peter Topping (in Y.A.J., No. 54)

The Kiplin Hall Archive NYCC 1989

Kiplin Hall, North Yorkshire — Richard Haslam (Country Life 7/1983)

The Dalesmen of the Mississippi River (p.55) — David Morris (Sessions 1989)

CHAPTER XIV

The Life and Times of William I — Maurice Ashley (Weidenfeld & Nicholson 1973)

The Year of the Conquest — David Howarth (Callers 1977)

The Domesday Book — Edited by John Morris — Yorkshire Parts 1 & 2 (Phillimore 1986)

The Early History of the North Riding — William Edwards (A. Brown 1924)

CHAPTER XV

Golden Vale of Mowbray — Bogg (Elliot Stock 1909)

Topcliffe — M.D. Watson (C.B. Press, Thirsk)

CHAPTER XVI

Stapyltons of Yorkshire — Chetwynd Stapleton (Longmans Green 1987)

The Battles of Yorkshire — Leadman (Bradbury Agnew 1891)

Yorkshire Battles — Edward Lamplough (Andrews 1891)

Chapter Notes

1 Refer to The Harker Family — translation by E.C. Wright (Harrison 1932).
2 Records show that this was an ancient mill dating back to 1536 when it was let to Brian Clarkson and Ralph Peacock by the Lord of the Manor at 6/8d per annum.
3 NYCRO ZJ1/1/8-9.
4 The Chronicles of Lanercost, p.210.
5 Richmond and District Civic Society Review No.11, pgs.6/9.
6 The Green Bridge — L.P. Wenham.
7 The spelling of the name has been given other interpretations e.g. Hindrelaghe and Hindrelac but, in his editing of the Yorkshire section of the Domesday Book, John Morris clearly favoured Hindrelag which, as indicated, can be related to the Danish language.
8 Yorkshire Archaeological Society Record Series XXI, pgs. 16, 27, 69 and Richmond Coucher Book 1781-1812.
9 Richmond and District Civic Society Review No. 5, p.28.
10 Richmond and District Civic Society Review No. 3, p.18.
11 Cal Close Rolls 1337-9, pgs. 424-33; 1343-6, pgs.149-55 and SP12/117/38.
12 BM. Add.Ms. 34324 fol. 15.
13 Richmond and District Civic Society Reviews No.4, p.28; No. 7, p.21 and No. 12, p.22.
14 Lansdowne Mss. No. 26, p.22.
15 Cal. Sp. Dom. 1651-2, p.470.
16 Though this name is assumed to be correct, it is quoted as Robert Swale in some records.
17 Richmond and District Civic Society Review No.8, p.40.
18 Letters and Papers of Henry VIII 1537 No.416.
19 YAJ No. 20, p.218 and Documents re Chapel of St. Ann — Sir J. Lawson.
20 YAJ No. 37, p.402.
21 The Dalesman No. 21 (Dalesman Diaries).
22 YAJ. 22, p.340.
23 Bede believed the date of consecration to be 21 July 625.

Index

139